*King's College Chapel, Cambridge.*

*Shire County Guide 23*

# CAMBRIDGESHIRE
## and Cambridge

Ronald Russell

Shire Publications Ltd

## CONTENTS

Printed in Great Britain by C. I. Thomas & Sons (Haverfordwest) Ltd, Press Buildings, Merlins Bridge, Haverfordwest, Dyfed SA61 1XF.
British Library Cataloguing in Publication Data available.

ACKNOWLEDGEMENTS
The photographs on pages 1, 29, 31, 35, 41 and 46 are by Cadbury Lamb. Other photographs including the cover, are by the author. The maps (pages 12, 47 and 69) are by D. R. Darton.

Cover: *Ely Cathedral.*

Below: *The gatehouse of Buckden Palace, former residence of the Bishops of Lincoln.*

*The river Great Ouse, near the Hemingfords.*

# 1
# A county of contrasts

Cambridgeshire is a greedy county. Over the years it has absorbed the Isle of Ely, the Soke of Peterborough and the county of Hunting-donshire. It looks enviously at Newmarket to the south-east and Royston to the south. So far it has failed to obtain an area of coastline, but who is to say what a future reorganisation of local government might decree? So here is a county divided from its neighbours by artificial lines rather than by natural barriers, with a widely varied geological structure, with no special architectural character of its own, with much of its area at or below mean sea level, with one of the world's most beautiful cities as its county town and with a countryside as little known and appreciated as that of any county in England.

Tourists flock to Cambridge, about three million a year. Some of them penetrate to Ely but few adventure elsewhere except possibly to the National Trust properties of Wimpole Hall and Anglesey Abbey. Peterborough attracts visitors to events at the East of England Showground, but the surrounding countryside is virtually undiscovered territory. The huge flat fields and straight watercourses may not look enticing. This is a working countryside with no concessions or allowances made for visitors and tourists unless they want

to buy fruit and vegetables or pick their own strawberries. There are few hotels, even in Cambridge itself, and only a small handful of hospitable farmhouses and bed and breakfast establishments.

So, Cambridge apart, what does the county have to offer? Perhaps the best way to answer this is to look at how the county is made up, to examine briefly the different regions of which it is composed, and then to look in more detail at the nature reserves, the cathedrals and churches, the historic buildings, the individual towns and villages, and everything else that goes to make Cambridgeshire, as Rupert Brooke wrote, 'of all England, the shire for men who understand'.

The greatest contrast in Cambridgeshire is between the north and south. In the northern-most part, around Wisbech, are the silt fens. In early prehistoric times the land extended much further into the North Sea than it does today. Very slowly the level of the land began to sink and gradually the sea took over, depositing first the peat and then the silt which eventually covered the fenland to a depth of many feet. The relatively stable silt attracted settlers and in time developed into rich farm-ing land, the wealth of which may be seen in the grandeur of some of the churches built in

3

medieval times.

South-west of the silt fens is the larger area of peat fen with islands rising above it. For several centuries men strove to drain these fens which were subject to constant flooding from the many rivers wandering across them. The Romans, the great religious foundations, landowners and farmers all left their mark on the landscape. Monasteries and convents were established on the islands, at Ely, Ramsey and Chatteris for example, some later to develop into wealthy abbeys, owning large tracts of land.

South and east of the peat fens is the land of the fen edge. On this firmer ground, just above fen level, settlements developed, some of them linking with the larger rivers by means of canals or lodes, thus becoming small inland ports. Stone quarried in and around the fen edge, notably Barnack Rag from the west and clunch from the Burwell area, was used in the building of many of the churches and Cambridge colleges in medieval times.

Much of the southern half of the county is chalk downland with gentle hills rising to a height of about 400 feet (120 metres). In the south-east corner towards the Essex border there is a band of clay and in the south-west a clay plateau once covered by forest. Most of Huntingdonshire District in the west is upland clay, although the peat fen extends into the north-east region and there is a band of limestone in the far north. There are bands of alluvial gravels along the natural courses of the Great Ouse and the Nene.

The varied landscape helps to account for the patterns of settlement in early years and for the marked contrasts in the Cambridgeshire countryside. Pre-Roman settlements for the most part have been discovered on the fen edge and islands and close to the courses of the larger rivers. These same sites are those which it seems the Romans preferred, although there was also a movement into the western clay region and into the valley of the Cam. More research is needed before the whole picture is revealed.

Roman attempts to prevent flooding and improve drainage influenced the landscape, especially the construction of Car Dyke and two at least of the Cambridgeshire lodes (see chapters 3 and 4). The Romans created a busy industrial town west of Peterborough, the pottery-manufacturing centre known as *Durobrivae,* and a Roman town grew up around the road junction at Godmanchester. There was also a scattering of forts and villas, but the county is not rich in Roman remains.

Saxon settlers moved into Cambridgeshire during the fifth and sixth centuries and the great earthworks known as the dykes were constructed, it seems, in this period. They lie

*On the silt fen near Leverington.*

4

*South-west Cambridgeshire: in the foreground is the site of the lost village of Clopton.*

across the line of the Icknield Way, the ancient trackway from Wessex to Norfolk, as if to block invaders from the south-west, although their exact purpose and date are not yet known.

In the seventh century came the earliest of the Christian foundations: in 647 the monastery at Soham, founded by St Felix; in 664 the monastery at Medeshamstede, or Peterborough, shortly followed by a monastery at Thorney; and in 673 a community of monks and nuns at Ely, founded by Etheldreda, daughter of King Anna of East Anglia, who became its abbess. All these foundations were destroyed by the Danes, who occupied much of East Anglia for about fifty years in the late ninth and early tenth centuries, but all except Soham rose again to become richer, more powerful and more influential. Ramsey, the other great religious foundation, was dedicated in 974.

These abbeys, as they became, were major landowners. They founded, or appropriated, churches throughout the county, opened daughter houses, and it was a Bishop of Ely who was largely responsible for the foundation of Cambridge as a collegiate university.

During medieval times there was a general expansion and extension of settlement throughout the county. Woodlands were cleared, waste lands were cultivated and farmers moved to reclaimed land on the silt fens and the islands in the peat. The so-called

Roman bank or wall to the north of Wisbech dates from this period, a flood barrier with the reclaimed land to the west.

It was also during this period that a major change in the pattern of the rivers in the county took place. The Nene, Ouse and Ouse tributaries meandered across the fenland, their courses shifting and changing with flood water from the uplands and incursions from the sea. In particular an arm of the Ouse, known variously as the West Water, Well Stream or Wisbech Ouse, wandered across the flat lands from near Littleport to Wisbech and an outfall into the Wash. This outfall silted up and gradually the river disappeared. The course of this and other abandoned watercourses can be traced by roddons, the lines of old river beds often discernible by aerial photography as lighter bands now raised above the level of the wasted peat fens.

In the fourteenth century an economic recession affected most of the county, compounded by the plague of 1348-50 which led, it is estimated, to a 39 per cent reduction in the population. Some smaller villages virtually disappeared and others were much reduced in size. The recovery which followed led to the growth of a new class of yeoman farmers, many of whom soon became wealthy and began the process of enclosure. Some of the old churches were rebuilt or extended and many of the county's larger houses were constructed, culminating in 1640 with the building of Cambridgeshire's grandest mansion, Wimpole Hall.

Following this economic recovery three major events influenced the development of the county. First the Dissolution of the Monasteries by Henry VIII led to the destruction of Ramsey, Thorney, St Ives, Anglesey, the nunneries of Chatteris and Swaffham, St Edmund's Priory in Cambridge and Denny Abbey, and the sequestration of their wealth and estates. Secondly, in the mid seventeenth century, came the draining of the fens by the Dutch engineer, Cornelius Vermuyden, for the immediate benefit of the Earl of Bedford and his fellow adventurers, which drastically altered the fenland landscape and led to increased prosperity for the landowners. Thirdly was the period of Parliamentary enclosures, from 1770 to about 1850, when the common fields and open pasture were transformed into the regulated countryside of today.

Since the Second World War there have been further changes in the landscape. In the rich fenland areas farms have become larger, hedges have been grubbed up and trees cut down in the interests of greater productivity and increased profits. Many of the farmers no longer own their farms, which belong to City institutions or investment companies. Intensive cultivation and improved drainage have wasted the peat, with the result that in places it is near to disappearing and the chalk beneath is showing through. Further wastage is caused by the occasional fen blow when strong winds tear across the flat fields now unprotected by hedges or shelter belts. Unless the danger signals are observed and acted upon the outcome could be disastrous.

The population of Cambridgeshire is growing. The M11 motorway has greatly improved the connection with London and the railway is electrified. New 'high tech' industries in and around Cambridge and Peterborough and science and business parks in various villages are proving attractive and there is little unemployment in the county. In Cambridge and the surrounding villages housing is under pressure and prices are continually rising. Bar Hill, a new village 3 miles (5 km) west of Cambridge, is fully developed and there are plans for further new villages. In the Peterborough area there has been enormous expansion with nearly six hundred new factories and warehouses being constructed on Development Corporation sites and large housing estates engulfing the villages nearby. With a few exceptions in remoter parts of the fenland, there is a general air of prosperity in the county. Handsomely restored cottages line the streets of many of the southern villages and there are plenty of glossy, well equipped, locally owned cruisers on the Ouse.

The prosperity of Cambridge and Peterborough is reflected elsewhere in the county. In the Ouse valley St Neots and St Ives have both expanded and the riverside villages are so developed that it is hard to see where one ends and the next begins. Ely has extended to the north and west and publicity for the cathedral's restoration appeal seems to have attracted extra visitors. The port of Wisbech has been updated and the town is usually alive with bustling activity. March, however, has lost its huge railway marshalling yards and the small fen towns of Chatteris and Littleport (which has lost its secondary school) present their usual dour faces to a mostly unappreciative world.

This is a county of contrasts and to understand and appreciate it properly needs more than just a token sampling. Forget Cambridge for a time; it is not Cambridgeshire any more than Stratford-upon-Avon is Warwickshire. Forget Peterborough, too; like any new town it does not represent the county in which it has been planted. Instead try some of the class B and minor roads and see what they reveal.

**Itineraries for motorists**

It is helpful to divide the county into areas, any one of which can be comfortably explored by car in four to six hours, allowing time to enter churches and stroll along village streets.

In the northern part of the county Wisbech makes a good starting point and a circular tour taking in Leverington, Newton, Gorefield, Parson Drove, Guyhirn, Coldham, Friday Bridge and Elm makes a valuable introduction to the silt fens with time to enjoy Wisbech itself.

From Peterborough two areas can be explored. To the east is the North Level via Whittlesey, Thorney, Newborough, Peakirk, Northborough and Maxey, returning through Helpston and Glinton. The countryside to the west is of very different character with the villages of Marholm, Ufford and Barnack, then southward to Wansford and Water Newton, returning through Castor and Longthorpe.

Ramsey is a useful place to begin a tour of Huntingdonshire, by heading westward over the fens through Holme and across the A1 to Glatton, the Giddings, Winwick, Hamerton, Leighton Bromswold, Buckworth and the Alconburys, returning through Wood Walton, Great Raveley and Upwood. From Huntingdon or Godmanchester one can travel west to Grafham Water and Kimbolton and return through St Neots to discover the Ouse valley and the Offords, the Hemingfords, Houghton and St Ives.

West and south-west of Cambridge there is a profusion of pleasant villages but any tour in

6

*New industrial architecture near Cambridge.*

this direction should include the Gransdens, Gamlingay, Orwell, Bourn, Toft and Comberton. To the south are Harlton, Barrington, Shepreth and Melbourn, Fowlmere, Thriplow, Duxford and Whittlesford, and to the southeast Linton, Balsham, Westley Waterless, Brinkley, Burrough Green, Dullingham, Wood Ditton and the other villages around Newmarket, returning through the Wilbrahams and Fulbourn.

This leaves the fen edge with the B1102 joining Stow-cum-Quy, Lode, Swaffham Bulbeck, Swaffham Prior, Burwell and Fordham. Lastly comes Ely for the villages of the Isle, Little Downham, Mepal, Sutton, Haddenham, Wilburton, Stretham, Wicken, Soham, Isleham and Prickwillow.

Many other places of interest remain, in the fens, the Huntingdon uplands, the borders with Suffolk, the lands of clay and chalk. This is a richly varied county with much to offer, much to be enjoyed.

*Wicken Fen, showing the restored wind pump.*

# 2
# The countryside

There is comparatively little open accessible countryside in Cambridgeshire and less woodland than in any other English county. What there is, however, has been carefully preserved and there is much to interest the natural history enthusiast. Some forty nature reserves are administered by the Cambridgeshire Wildlife Trust and several more in Huntingdon District are in the care of the Bedfordshire and Huntingdonshire Naturalists' Trust. Admission to most of these reserves is restricted to Trust members but there is free public access to some while permission may be sought to visit certain others. The Trust's address is 5 Fulbourn Manor, Fulbourn, Cambridge CB1 5BN; telephone 0223 990788.

## NATURE RESERVES (open to the public)
**Beechwood Reserve,** near Cambridge (OS 154: TL 486548). South of the road between Worts Causeway and Fulbourn.
There are 12 acres (5 ha) of mature beech with an old chalk pit. The white helleborine may be found here.

**Buff Wood Nature Reserve,** Hatley St George (OS 153: TL 283509).
There is public access to the northern part of the wood from the eastern end of the village. For access to the whole wood apply to the Director, Botanical Gardens, University of Cambridge.

**Gamlingay Cinques** (OS 153: TL 226529).
A remnant of a large heath, Gamlingay Common, and once used as a sand pit, the Cinques is a series of wet hollows with a wide variety of plants not found elsewhere in the county.

**Roswell Pits Nature Trail,** Ely (OS 153: TL 547805).
The trail leads around old clay pits now used for sailing and angling. The area is notable for bird life — kingfishers and great crested grebes nest here — and for insects and a wide variety of flora.

**Wandlebury** (OS 154: TL 493533). 4 miles (6.5 km) south-east of Cambridge on A604.
This popular wooded area of 109 acres (44 ha) incorporates a length of Roman road and the site of an iron age fort (see chapter 4). A helpful guide to the area is available on the site.

**WOODLAND RESERVES (permits required)**
**Fulbourn Fen,** Fulbourn (OS 154: TL 515580).

This is an educational nature reserve with 67 acres (27 ha) of woodland, grassland and scrub with a wide variety of trees and wild flowers.

**Hardwick Wood** (OS 154: TL 354572). Off the road from Hardwick to Toft, south of A45.

The wood, now 40 acres (16 ha) in extent, is recorded in Doomsday Book and for several centuries belonged to the Bishops of Ely; hence its history is well documented. It contains forty species of trees and shrubs and about 130 species of other plants and ferns.

**Hayley Wood,** near Little Gransden (OS 153: TL 294534). Just south of B1046.

This 122 acre (50 ha) wood has a recorded history of seven hundred years and is especially rich in wildlife with deer, foxes, hares and rabbits, a wide variety of birds and over 280 species of flowering plants and ferns. Oak, ash, maple, hazel and hawthorn are the dominant trees. With its ancient hedges, huge ash-stools and enormous number of oxlips, this is a site of first importance and interest.

Other carefully preserved ancient woods are **Knapwell Wood,** 7 miles (11 km) west of Cambridge off A45 (OS 154: TL 333607), 11 acres (4.5 ha), notable for spring flowers, **Papworth Wood,** Papworth (OS 153: TL 292628), 18 acres (7 ha), also with a splendid display of spring flowers, and **Overhall Grove,** Knapwell (OS 154: TL 337633), 43 acres (17.5 ha), with some of the largest oaks in Britain. There are three small areas of woodland near Great Raveley, **Riddy Wood** near Wood Walton, **Waresley Wood,** Waresley, and **Gransden Wood,** Great Gransden. Further information can be obtained from the Cambridgeshire Wildlife Trust.

**NATIONAL NATURE RESERVES**

Permits are generally required to visit National Nature Reserves. These can be obtained from the Nature Conservancy Council, East Midlands Region, Northminster House, Peterborough PE1 1UA.

**Barnack Hills and Holes,** Barnack (OS 142: TF 077048).

In medieval times stone was extracted for cathedrals, churches and college buildings from quarries on this site on the outskirts of Barnack.

**Castor Hanglands** (OS 142: TF 120015). 2 miles north of Ailsworth.

This is a varied area of woodland, scrub, grassland and wetland.

**Holme Fen,** near Holme (OS 142: TL 205890). 6 miles south of Peterborough.

This reserve of about 638 acres (258 ha) of birch woodland lies on the south-west side of the site of Whittlesey Mere. Drained in 1851, the bed of the mere has been rich farmland for over a hundred years. Although most of Holme Fen is covered with silver birch, originally planted as shelter belts and game cover, there are still wetland areas and peat cutting has created two new meres of much importance for wildlife.

By the minor road to Holme Lode Farm are the Holme Fen posts (OS 142: TL 203894). In 1851 the original post was driven through the peat into the clay beneath until its top was level with the surface. The 13 feet (4 metres) of the post now visible show how much the peat has shrunk in the intervening years. The second post, installed in 1957, shows the level of the land at various dates. The posts are accessible to the public.

**Monks Wood,** Wood Walton (OS 142: TL 200800). 7 miles north-west of Huntingdon on B1090.

Much of this area of woodland has been wooded throughout recorded history. It is especially notable for the variety of butterflies and moths and there is also a wide range of plants including the bird's nest and greater butterfly orchid.

**Woodwalton Fen** (OS 142: TL 233850). 9 miles south-east of Peterborough in the Fenland.

This is one of the very few remnants of natural fen and is carefully managed to preserve the fenland habitat. There is a wide variety of plant and insect life.

*The Holme Fen posts.*

9

*Peakirk Waterfowl Gardens are one of the two Wildfowl Trust reserves in Cambridgeshire.*

## OTHER SITES
### The Ouse Washes

There are three nature reserves in the Ouse Washes, the area between the Old and New Bedford rivers into which water overflows in time of flood. Two of the reserves are at **Welches Dam,** south-west of Manea (OS 143: TL 478871), where the Royal Society for the Protection of Birds and the Cambridgeshire Wildlife Trust share a visitors' centre. Several hides are open to members of these organisations. Further north at **Welney** (OS 143: TL 539933) is the 850 acre (344 ha) Wildfowl Trust Refuge with an observatory overlooking a lagoon which is floodlit on winter evenings. Among the birds to be seen on the Washes are ruff, black-tailed godwit, redshank, lapwing and snipe. Thousands of Bewick's swans winter at Welney as well as several varieties of duck, including shelduck, garganey, gadwall, pintail, teal, shoveller, mallard, pochard and tufted duck. In summer there are conducted evening walks at the Wildfowl Refuge. For details contact the Warden, Wildfowl Trust, Pintail House, Welney; telephone 0353 860711.

**Peakirk Waterfowl Gardens,** Peakirk, near Peterborough. Telephone: 0733 252271. Wildfowl Trust. Off B1443, 5 miles (8 km) north of Peterborough.

Cambridgeshire is the only county with two Wildfowl Trust reserves. Peakirk has 17 acres (7 ha) of waterfowl gardens created from old gravel workings that were later used as osier beds. The Roman canal, Car Dyke, runs through the site which is divided into several ponds with separate pens for more aggressive birds or species which need special protection. There are about eighty varieties of wildfowl here, including eight different breeds of swan (trumpeters, whoopers, Bewick's, black-necked, black, Coscoroba, mute and whistling) and thirty breeds of geese. A special attraction is a flock of Chilean flamingoes. Many woodland birds may also be seen.

**Wicken Fen** (OS 154: TL 563705). National Trust. ½ mile (0.8 km) south-west of Wicken village, clearly signposted from the A1123.

This vitally important wetland reserve is open throughout the year. It consists of Wicken Sedge Fen (330 acres; 133.5 ha), St Edmund's Fen (55 acres; 22.25 ha) and, on the far side of Wicken Lode, Adventurers' Fen (220 acres; 89 ha). The National Trust first purchased part of the Fen in 1899 and has acquired the rest piece by piece since. At one time peat, sedge, hay and reeds were harvested here and when this ceased, scrub and woodland developed over much of the area. Now the Trust manages the Fen with the aim of maintaining and preserving the enormous diversity of plant and insect life for which Wicken is internationally famous.

Buildings on the property include the William Thorpe Building, with an explanatory display on the wildlife and management of the reserve, the Ganges Hut, used as a dormitory

10

for working parties and schools, and a restored wind pump (see chapter 8). Two trails have been laid out: a nature trail and a shorter boardwalk trail which may be used by wheelchairs and push-chairs. The fen is now several feet above the level of the surrounding countryside, having been almost unaffected by the drainage of past years. A high water table has to be maintained and waterproof footwear is necessary everywhere except on the boardwalk trail.

Wicken Lode serves for drainage and is also navigable by light craft. Adventurers' Fen has been drained and cultivated in the past but since becoming National Trust property in 1950 it has been maintained for the benefit of wildlife. The mere was created in 1955.

## WALKING IN CAMBRIDGESHIRE

There are several hundred miles of footpath in the southern half of the county and signposting and clearing of rights of way are gradually leading to improvement. The gentle contours make walking easy. In the fens there are few paths and those that exist mostly run in straight lines along the edges of fields. A good fenland walk is along the haling way of Burwell Lode, while the footpath along Devil's Dyke (access at Reach, or from the A45 at OS 154: TL 619614) gives a fascinating 7½ miles (12 km) of changing views and perspectives.

In 1980 a middle-distance walk, the Wimpole Way, was established. This leaves Cam-bridge at the junction of Adams Road and Wilberforce Road and is waymarked via the villages of Coton, Caldecote and Kingston to Wimpole, a distance of 11 miles (17.7 km). There is a bus service for the return journey. Another popular walk is along the so-called Roman Road, a green lane from Horseheath to Wandlebury with a further 2 miles (3.2 km) to a bus stop by Addenbrooke's Hospital, a total distance of 10 miles (16 km). The best-known walk in the Cambridge area, however, is the riverside stroll from Mill Lane to Grantchester, just over 4 miles (6.5 km) return.

The Peterborough area is better served for walks than might at first appear. An excellent series of free leaflets describing several country walks is obtainable from the City Planning Department, Town Hall, Peterborough, or from the Tourist Information Office (chapter 12).

A long-distance footpath keeping close to the Great Ouse runs from Bluntisham to St Neots, passing through Needingworth, Holywell, Houghton, Godmanchester and Little Paxton. A descriptive leaflet of this Ouse Valley Trail can be obtained from Huntingdonshire District Council, Huntingdon, or from local museums and tourist information offices.

For further information about walking in the county, contact the Ramblers Association, 1/5 Wandsworth Road, London SW8 2XX; telephone 01-582 6878.

*The Ouse Washes in time of flood.*

11

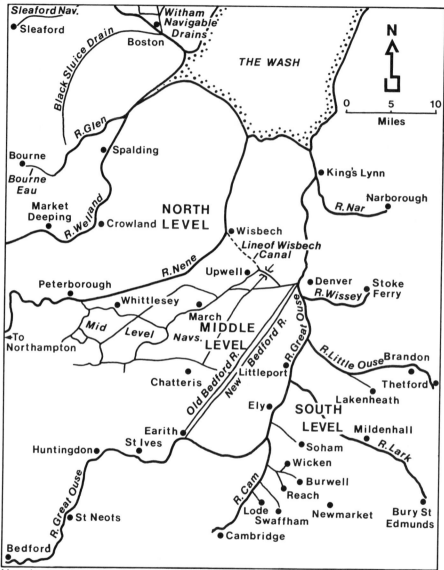

*Map showing the principal rivers and waterways of the Fenland.*

12

*Orton Lock on the river Nene near Peterborough.*

# 3
# The Fenland:
# drainage and waterways

## Drainage

Most of north and east Cambridgeshire is fenland, in early times 'an arm of the sea', with habitation around the edges and on 'islands' here and there. With the falling of the sea level more land became available for cultivation and during the Roman occupation energetic efforts were made to control flooding, drain the land and encourage agriculture. The Car Dyke (see chapter 4) is the major surviving undertaking of those times. Following the departure of the Romans spasmodic attempts were made, mainly by the various wealthy religious houses, to continue and extend their work, including the creation in the thirteenth century of a massive earthwork around the Wash and the construction of various drains and river diversions, of which Morton's Leam, a new course of the Nene between Peterborough and Guyhirn made to the orders of Bishop Morton about 1490, is an important example.

The great undertaking which changed the face of the countryside, however, was the drainage operation of the mid seventeenth century. This was financed by the Earl of Bedford and a group of fellow adventurers (as they were known), who were to receive 95,000 acres (38,500 ha) of drained land in return for their sponsorship and management of the scheme. The area to be drained was known as the Great or Bedford Level and the engineer in charge was the Dutchman Cornelius Ver-

muyden. He divided the Level into three parts, the names of which still survive: the North Level, from the River Glen to Morton's Leam; the Middle Level, from the Leam to the Great Ouse; and the South Level, from the Ouse to the fen edge. Work took place in two main stages, interrupted by the Civil War. Vermuyden's method was to cut a number of straight drains on as steep a gradient as he could find, with sluices at the northern ends to keep out the sea. Of these drains the New and Old Bedford rivers, cutting diagonally across the Middle Level for about 20 miles (32 km) with the flood reservoir of the Ouse Washes between them, are the most ambitious and impressive. Other major works included the Twenty Foot, Forty Foot and Sixteen Foot drains, the restoration of Popham's Eau of 1605, and the building of the massive sluice at Denver. Vermuyden also intended to make a sweeping catchwater drain to take off the surplus water of the Ouse tributaries, but funds were insufficient and the idea had to wait until the mid twentieth century before it was realised.

Vermuyden's scheme was largely successful but it brought various unforeseen complications with it. The flow of the watercourses was too weak to clear the silt brought in by the tides and problems developed at Denver and the other sluices. More seriously, the peat topsoil which covered most of the drained

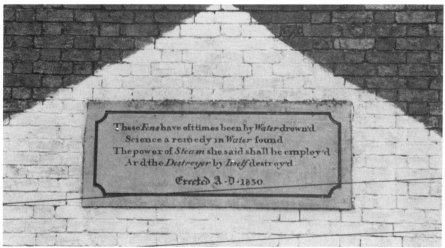

*An inscription at Hundred Foot pumping station in the Fens.*

lands shrank and wasted as it dried out, leading to a lowering in the level of the land. This made drainage by gravity impossible and also resulted in the weakening of the raised banks of the drains and hence to increased flooding. It became necessary to install wind pumps to lift water from smaller to larger drains, and by the eighteenth century several hundred were at work in the fens. Then in 1713 Denver sluice collapsed; it took 35 years before it was replaced, years of fierce controversy between the navigators, who did not want the sluice, and the drainers, who did. During this period there were two improvements to the river Nene: the cutting of a new channel in 1728, Smith's Leam, between Peterborough and Guyhirn (this is the present channel), and the making of Kindersley's Cut near the river outfall into the Wash, which improved the drainage of the North Level.

Many developments took place during the nineteenth century, including the replacement of wind pumps by steam engines, the construction of the Middle Level Main Drain, the draining of the inland lakes known as meres, and the improvement of the outfalls of the Great Ouse and the Nene. Most of the great engineers of the time were involved with the fenland in one way or another. However, there was no general oversight of the situation; the rivers themselves were treated in sections and the internal drainage bodies operated independently. Overall assessment of the problems was impossible and improvements in one area sometimes led to deterioration elsewhere.

Not until 1930 were steps taken to co-ordinate and control the situation. The Land Drainage Act led to the setting up of Catchment Boards for each of the major rivers. Now work affecting the whole of a river and its catchment area could be undertaken and investigations into the basic causes of flooding and the effectiveness of the total drainage pattern were begun. The boards were later replaced by River Authorities and these are now part of the Anglian Water Authority. Major floods in 1936 and 1937 showed the urgency of the problem. Some solutions were devised by the engineers Murdoch Macdonald and Partners but in 1947 the greatest fen flood of recorded times occurred with 37,000 acres (15,000 ha) being inundated in the South Level alone. Eventually a cut-off channel around the south-eastern fen edge and a relief channel for the Ouse below Denver were constructed — two proposals originally advanced by Vermuyden. New and more powerful pumping stations were erected and various improvements and modifications were made in the Middle Level. With the completion of these works it now seems that the fens are at last effectively drained.

## Waterways

Nature and the fen drainers have left Cambridgeshire with a considerable mileage of waterway, much of which is navigable. For centuries the fens depended almost entirely upon water transport, especially for heavier goods. The great fairs of Stourbridge and St Ives were mainly supplied by water; stone for the cathedrals, abbeys, churches and many of the Cambridge colleges came by water; farm

14

produce was shifted by water and in later years fuel for the pumping stations was delivered by water. Within the county Peterborough, Wisbech, March, Ramsey, Ely, Cambridge, St Ives, Huntingdon and St Neots were on water transport routes and there was a line of small inland ports — Soham, Burwell, Reach, Swaffham Bulbeck and Lode — along the fen edge. Before the building of Denver sluice small sea-going vessels could penetrate far inland, but after that time fenland lighters were developed. These were open boats, approximately 45 by 10 feet (13.5 by 3 metres), each capable of carrying about 25 tons which operated in gangs of between four and fourteen, hauled by a horse and later by a steam tug. Cargoes from overseas were transferred to lighters at King's Lynn.

Railway competition reduced the receipts of the lightermen and of the navigation commissioners with the result that maintenance fell into arrears and efficiency diminished. Some

*St Ives, a riverside town on the Great Ouse.*

traffic — notably in sugar beet, fertiliser, bricks, clunch (a soft, chalky stone used for building), gas water (a dirty black liquid effluent rich in ammonia for fertilisers) from Cambridge Gas Works, clay for bank repairs and peat — carried on until the Second World War, when the fenland was opened up to road transport by the concrete roads of the War Agricultural Executive Committees and commercial traffic on the waterways came to a halt.

Recently pleasure cruising has become popular in the fens and to some extent this is a revival of an old tradition. In 1774 Lord Orford wrote a diary of his voyage round the fens with a fleet of nine boats hauled by a fen horse called Hippopotamus. Regattas were frequently held on Whittlesey Mere. Sailing races took place on the Ouse in the early twentieth century and the Cambridge Motor Boat Club was founded in 1913. However, since the 1960s there has been a vast increase in the number of pleasure cruisers using the waterways, especially on the Great Ouse above Earith and near Ely. The Middle Level, with its straight drains and high banks, is less popular but connects the Great Ouse and Nene and both the Old Nene and Well Creek provide pleasant cruising waters. Boats can be hired by the week or fortnight from many places including Earith, Ely, St Ives and March and the waterways are seldom crowded except at Ely and at the locks between Earith and St Neots in the height of the summer season. If time allows it is possible to reach the canal system from the Great Ouse by crossing the Middle Level to the Nene and travelling upstream to Northampton where there is a canal connection to the Grand Union, the main line to London, Birmingham, Leicester and beyond.

Angling has always been a favourite fenland pursuit, originally to stock the larder but latterly for sport. Excellent coarse fishing is available on the Ouse, its tributaries and the Middle Level, and the Cut-Off and Relief Channels, neither open to boats, are well stocked. Pike, zander, bream, roach, perch and tench — and eels — are usually plentiful. The Fisheries Officer of the Anglian Water Authority, Chivers Way, Histon, Cambridge CB4 4ZY (telephone: 0223 235235), will provide full details.

15

*The foundations of a Roman barn in Ferry Meadows Country Park, near Peterborough.*

# 4
# Places of archaeological interest

**Car Dyke**

Sections of the Car Dyke catchwater drain in Cambridgeshire may be found alongside the A10 by the south-west boundary of Waterbeach airfield and across country between the A10 at grid reference TL 671481 and the B1049 at TL 692472. A good clear stretch, much of it in water, exists to the north of Peterborough across country from 1 mile (1.5 km) north-west of Eye on the A47 to Peakirk, where it runs through the Wildfowl Trust sanctuary (see chapter 2).

The drain was cut during the Roman occupation, probably in the third century AD. It linked the Cam just south of Waterbeach to the Great Ouse about 2 miles (3 km) above Twentypence Bridge on the Cottenham-Wilburton road and continued in a roughly north-westerly direction, circling north of Peterborough and eventually connecting with the River Witham near Lincoln, incorporating lengths of natural rivers on its route. The dyke was primarily for drainage but it is possible that it was also used as a navigable canal by which hides and grain could be transported from the rich farmlands of the fen edge to the legions in the north, the route continuing from the Witham via the Foss Dyke and the Trent to the Yorkshire Ouse. Some stretches may have been used by small vessels in medieval times.

**Devil's Dyke**

Three major earthworks were cut as defensive lines in or about the sixth century AD. They were ditches with embankments on the northern side, probably to deter invaders from the south-west. Devil's Dyke, running for 7½ miles (12 km) from Ditton Green to Reach, is the longest and the best preserved. In parts the distance from the bottom of the ditch to the top of the embankment is 30 feet (9.1 metres) and the width of the fortification is more than 100 feet (30.5 metres). For many centuries it marked the division between two East Anglian dioceses and it still marks the parish boundary between Burwell and Swaffham Prior. Along the embankment are some of the few areas of chalk grassland that survive in this region and conservation work is necessary to prevent its being overwhelmed by scrub. Several roads intersect the dyke and the path along the top is a right of way for walkers only.

**Fleam Dyke** is similar in construction but less impressive. The best surviving section is between Balsham and Fulbourn. A right of way runs along the top of the embankment and can be reached from the A11 just north of the crossroads with the Fulbourn-Balsham road. Fleam Dyke is a Site of Special Scientific Interest.

**Heydon** or **Bran Ditch** is the third of these

defensive works. It ran from Heydon to Fowlmere and the best place to inspect it is at the southern end, but much of this ditch has been obliterated.

A fourth ditch or dyke is **Brent Ditch,** near Pampisford, of which about 1½ miles (2.5 km) can be traced on either side of the A11. This was not a defensive work and may have been simply a boundary marker.

**Flag Fen,** Peterborough.

A bronze age village was built on a platform in a lake some three thousand years ago. The site is now covered by fenland and excavations to recover the wooden houses that composed the village are in hand. The foundations of these buildings are still preserved. During part of the year the site is open to visitors with guided tours and displays in the visitors' centre. A small-scale reconstruction of the village can be seen on the island in Flag Fen Mere.

Flag Fen is 2 miles (3.2 km) from Fengate, where extensive excavations revealed a succession of prehistoric and Roman settlements before the expansion of Peterborough covered the area. For information about visits to Flag Fen telephone 0945 700336.

**Roman roads**

The A14 Royston to Huntingdon road is on the line of Ermine Street. This road later developed into the Old North Road and the villages nearby moved on to the road, attracted by the trade that the highway brought with it. Replaced by the A1, the Old North Road is now only a by-road.

The Roman road from Horseheath to the Gog Magog Hills is a broad track that makes excellent walking. It is claimed to be a section of the *Via Devana,* a road said to run from Colchester via Cambridge and Godmanchester to Leicester and Chester. The A604 Cambridge-Huntingdon road is on this line.

A road known as Akeman Street (not to be confused with Akeman Street in Oxfordshire) ran from Arrington on Ermine Street towards Cambridge and thence to Ely and further north. Some sections are shown on the Ordnance Survey map.

**Wandlebury**

Four miles south-west of Cambridge are the Gog Magog Hills, a chalk outcrop so called because, it is said, semblances of the legendary giants were once cut into the turf. On the hill top is Wandlebury iron age fort, about 1000 feet (305 metres) in diameter, surrounded by a

bank and ditch. There was a settlement inside the rampart and huts and storage pits have been found during excavations. The fort was probably reconstructed twice in the fourth and first centuries BC and abandoned by the first century AD.

In the eighteenth century an inner rampart was destroyed when the Godolphin family extended their estate. The house has now disappeared but the two stable blocks built in 1780 remain, converted to private dwellings. The famous breeding stallion, the Godolphin Arabian, is buried beneath the cupola of the larger block. The whole site is now owned by the Cambridge Preservation Society and is open to the public. Nature trails are laid out and there are splendid tree plantations, many dating from the eighteenth century, and good views over Cambridge. A tea room and display room are on the site.

**Water Newton**

On the east side of this village by the A1 is the site of the Roman town of *Durobrivae*. The town, 44 acres (18 ha) in extent, grew up around the crossing of the river Nene by Ermine Street, which here coincides with the line of the A1 to the south. An important pottery industry developed and traces of kilns and workshops have been discovered as well as many examples of the pottery itself. The industry produced both everyday household wares and objects of high quality which were despatched to other parts of England. Output was at its height between the second and fourth centuries AD.

The site of a Roman fort guarding the Ermine Street river crossing has also been found. Across the river at Castor evidence of several Roman buildings has been discovered near the parish church and a Roman villa half a mile (800 metres) to the south-east was excavated in 1822. Further east at Longthorpe a fortress covering 27 acres (11 ha) was revealed by aerial photography in 1961 and training grounds for the troops have been excavated in Nene Park.

Many items excavated from these sites are on display in Peterborough Museum and the Museum of Archaeology in Cambridge. Two especially valuable collections are in the British Museum: a gold hoard and the Water Newton Silver. The silver objects, including bowls, flagons and cups, are marked with Christian symbols and are proof of the existence of Christianity in the Nene valley before the religion was officially recognised by the Romans.

*St Mary's church, Burwell.*

# 5
# Churches and cathedrals

Cambridgeshire is rich in churches although, possibly because they are overshadowed by the fame of the great cathedrals and college chapels, many of them are comparatively little known. There is no dominant style of church architecture but there is clear evidence of the influence of Ely's tower and octagon in several parishes across the county. There are some special glories: the angel roofs of March and Isleham, the towers of Barnack and Castor, Whittlesey's spire, the airy spaciousness of Burwell — these are all worth travelling miles to see. At Fletton there are unique Anglo-Saxon sculptures, while Great Paxton, Leighton Bromswold and Little Gidding are among churches of major historical interest. However, it is a sad reflection on present times that many of the churches are usually locked. A notice may tell you where to find the key; where this is not so, try the nearest cottage, the vicarage, local shop or pub. This is just a small selection of what may be found and enjoyed.

**Balsham:** Holy Trinity.
The large, dignified church stands in an extensive churchyard on the edge of the village. The thirteenth-century tower was strengthened in 1589 and fully restored in 1987. The late fourteenth-century nave and chancel stalls were provided by John de Sleaford, rector at that time. There are many unresolved architectural puzzles in this interesting building.

**Barnack:** St John Baptist.
Built of Barnack Rag, the local stone, the church has Saxon work in the lower stages of the tower and the tower arch and in a recess in the south aisle is a carved effigy of Christ dating from late Saxon times. Later centuries contributed much to this fine church, notably the massive thirteenth-century south porch, the fourteenth-century tracery in the chancel windows and the fifteenth-century Lady Chapel.

**Buckden:** St Mary.
The mostly fifteenth-century embattled church contrasts fascinatingly with the Great Tower of Buckden Palace, its close neighbour. Inside, the plaster has been stripped away,

except in the chancel; this darkens the interior and makes the arcade look surprisingly flimsy. There are memorials to three Bishops of Lincoln, the most striking being the large white marble lady on her knees reading the Bible, commemorating Bishop Pelham (died 1827) and dominating the north aisle.

**Burwell:** St Mary.

This is a splendid Perpendicular building, the interior flooded with light, handsomely proportioned, a real treasure. The delicately modelled stonework is mostly Burwell clunch with Barnack stone as a base. The oak roofs of nave and chancel are especially fine with carved cornices embellished with lively allegorical illustrations (but you need binoculars to see the detail). The likely mason/architect was Reginald Ely, who was responsible for part of King's College chapel and Queens' College gateway. The tower is older than the body of the church with evidence of Saxon and Norman work; the upper stage is reminiscent of the west tower of Ely and was probably added when the nave and chancel were built in 1464. St Mary's is a noble building with style and craftsmanship outstanding for a village church.

**Cambridge:** St Benet.

With the possible exception of Great Paxton, this is the oldest church in Cambridgeshire, with the tower and some other elements dating from the first half of the eleventh century. Note especially the tower arch with its comical lions and the handsome nave arcade of about 1300. A beautiful and highly atmospheric little churchyard separates St Benet's from Corpus Christi College, whose chapel it was until 1579. There is a remarkable list of over one hundred incumbents, most of them Fellows of Corpus, beginning in 1197.

**Cambridge:** St Botolph.

The west door beneath the fifteenth-century tower opens directly on to Trumpington Street and the calm, if rather severe, interior provides a refuge from the bustle outside. Most of the church is fourteenth-century, replacing a much older building. Notable are the 1647 font cover of painted wood and several interesting memorials, including one to the architect James Essex and a remarkably hideous one to Dr Thomas Plaifere, 1609, in the south chapel. The four bells were cast in 1460 and have been untouched since.

**Cambridge:** St Edward.

Hidden away in a small square with bookshops and the Arts Theatre restaurant, this is a richly historic church that has survived several changes and restorations. It was built in 1175 and almost entirely rebuilt in 1400, with

chancel aisles added in 1446 to provide chapels for Trinity Hall and Clare College. These aisles and seating were removed in the early 1930s to produce the unusually wide space around the altar. Note the chancel roof of 1400 and the fragile-looking early sixteenth-century pulpit used by the great reformer Hugh Latimer. Two translators of the Authorised Version of the Bible are buried here. The miniature churchyard by the west door is very attractive.

**Cambridge:** Holy Sepulchre (Round Church).

A favourite with tourists, the Round Church dates from about 1130 and was built to resemble the Holy Sepulchre in Jerusalem. It was heavily restored in 1841, when many of the earlier features were replaced, and the interior seems rather sanitised and has lost any sense of antiquity. Nevertheless, no tour of Cambridge is complete without a visit to the Round Church.

**Cambridge:** St Mary the Great.

This is the university church, the successor to a building of 1205 that was largely destroyed by fire. Rebuilding began in 1478 and continued piecemeal for over a hundred years. The result is a formal and dignified church with an especially fine roof of oak timbers given by Henry VII, well proportioned galleries installed in 1735, and a Victorian pulpit mounted on rails so that it can be moved into a central position for university sermons — the carved panels forming the screen come from an early Georgian pulpit which the present one replaced. The fine tower is not overwhelmed by the splendour of the buildings opposite and an ascent reveals a rewarding view over the city.

**Castor:** St Kyneburgha.

Kyneburgha was a daughter of Penda, king of Mercia. With her sister, Kyneswitha, she founded a nunnery at Castor in AD650 and this is the only church dedicated to her. It is a large, finely proportioned, handsome building with much Norman work, including the splendid tower, the north transept and the west end of the nave, all dating from 1124. The stubby spire was added about 1300. Almost all the rest is of the thirteenth and fourteenth centuries. There are some interesting small sculptures, inside and out, including a Saxon carving in the south wall of the chancel. The large east window floods the building with light. Note especially the columns in the crossing with decorated capitals, the coloured angels in the nave roof and the figures in the aisle roofs, and the impressive fourteenth-century south door with its large key on the inside. Outside see the carved decoration above the small door into the chancel and step back to admire the tower, floodlit at night.

The six bells were made by Henry Bagley of Ecton in 1700.

**Croydon:** All Saints.

This delightful little country church was built on an unstable site, as can be seen from the angles of the walls and arcades. It dates mainly from the fourteenth and fifteenth centuries apart from the chancel, rebuilt about 1685. There is little decoration; all is simple and peaceful. Sir George Downing, founder of Downing College, is buried in the vaults.

Much of the original village is deserted and one mile (1.6 km) south-west, accessible by a bridle path by the junction of the Croydon road with the road to Hatley, is the deserted village of Clopton, enclosed about 1495. Here were a church, mill and several houses. Although part of the site has been quarried and part ploughed up many of the outlines may still be traced.

*All Saints' church, Elm.*

**Doddington:** St Mary.

This was once a very important fenland parish, extensive and wealthy, with March among its daughter churches. Recent history has bypassed it, however. St Mary's is mainly late fourteenth-century, a substantial, compact building. There are good fifteenth-century windows in the chancel and a fine restored roof with angels, but very high, and the interior is dark. In the north aisle are a William Morris window and a Victorian grisaille window of two lights.

**Elm:** All Saints.

All Saints was dedicated in 1343 but the splendid tower is some sixty years older. Since then there has been little alteration or remodelling and the architecture has an unusual quality of harmony. The west end of the church, where there are no pews, is especially atmospheric. A few of the angels on the double hammerbeam roof have survived. The churchyard, with old trees and carefully carved headstones, is no less atmospheric. There are some fine eighteenth-century houses in the village and the frontage of the Black Horse Inn is worth studying.

**Ely:** Cathedral Church of the Holy and Undivided Trinity and St Etheldreda.

'The great ship of the Fens', like a massive Noah's ark grounded on a hill when the waters receded, was mostly completed by 1189. St Etheldreda, Queen of Northumbria, founded a religious community in Ely in AD 673 and was herself installed as abbess. The inscribed base of a cross in the south aisle commemorating Etheldreda's steward Ovin (Ovin's stone) is the only material link surviving from those times. Subsequent centuries saw Danish invasions, the refounding of Ely as a Benedictine monastery and the appropriation of much of its wealth as a penalty for supporting Hereward the Wake. In 1081 Abbot Simeon, finding the existing church inadequate, began an ambitious rebuilding. In 1109 the diocese of Ely was created. Pilgrims began to flock to Etheldreda's shrine (destroyed in the Reformation) and Bishop Hugh enlarged the church by building the splendid presbytery. In 1321 another major element, the Lady Chapel, was begun. In the following year, however, the central tower collapsed. The sacrist, Alan of Walsingham, determined to fill the open space thus created by a great octagon, crowned by a lantern designed by William Hurley, the King's Master Carpenter. Bishop Hotham restored the choir and Prior Crauden added the delightful chapel outside which bears his name. Other additions of the time were the belfry on top of the west tower and the beautiful chantry chapels of Bishop Alcock and Bishop West.

Above: *Ely Cathedral, showing the great west tower.*
Right: *Prior Crauden's Chapel in Ely Cathedral precincts.*

The interior, especially the Lady Chapel, suffered much damage after the Reformation and in the following two centuries the fabric seriously decayed. James Essex carried out many repairs after 1750 but the major restoration took place in the mid nineteenth century under Sir Gilbert Scott. This included adding pinnacles to the octagon and the installation of the painted ceiling in the nave. The west tower has subsequently been repaired and a restoration programme is in progress.

Among the cathedral's special glories are the superb west front, the Galilee Porch, the enormously long Norman nave, the unique octagon and lantern (binoculars help to discern the detail of the lantern paintings), the Romanesque work in the south-west transept, the intricate stonework of the chantry chapels and many of the monuments, the glorious Lady Chapel — a huge, light space, elegant and daring in conception — the choir stalls and their canopies. Do not miss Ovin's stone or the slate inscription in the presbytery where Etheldreda's shrine once stood, or the poem 'The Spiritual Railway' inscribed on a monument in the cloister to two men killed in a railway accident in 1845:

'. . . Come then poor Sinners, now's the time
At any Station on the line,

*The nave arcades at Holy Trinity church, Great Paxton.*

If you'll repent and turn from sin
The Train will stop and take you in.'
Go through the door in the south aisle and turn to examine the carving of Christ in Majesty, dating from about 1135. Re-enter and use the Monks' Door out to the largest assemblage of medieval buildings in England; and return to share the impact of entry with the thousands of monks who used this entrance centuries ago. The cathedral has a well stocked shop, an excellent café and, in the north triforium, the unique stained glass museum (see chapter 7). There is an admission charge to the building.

**Fletton:** St Margaret.
Hidden away in what is now a rather run-down suburb of Peterborough is this outstanding Norman church. Unfortunately it was not sufficiently hidden to escape arson in 1983; much of the chancel was fire-damaged and the nave was blackened by smoke. Good repair work has been done and the church is now bright and clean with an interesting new chancel roof. The chief treasure is a group of small Anglo-Saxon sculptures removed in 1981 from the chancel buttresses and now placed beneath the sill of the east window. They date from the early ninth century and show little animals, birds and patterns; one segment has three human heads. There is nothing to parallel them either in Britain or elsewhere.

Also in the chancel are two panels with saints, brought inside the church in 1901; these probably date from the early twelfth century. Much of St Margaret's is Norman, including the north arcade and the chancel arch; most of the rest is late thirteenth/early fourteenth-century. Outside by the west tower is an Anglo-Saxon cross with a Norman inscription, 'Radulph Filius Wilielmi'.

**Great Paxton:** Holy Trinity.
From outside this seems a pleasant, ordinary fourteenth- to fifteenth-century village church. It is, however, a rarity: one of the very few surviving cruciform Saxon churches dating from the early eleventh century. Note the nave arcades, the north transept arch and the round-headed clerestory windows — all pre-Conquest. Almost all the rest of the building is Perpendicular. The interior is light and fresh, both impressive and appealing. A sad note is struck by a handwritten notice: 'Everything of value in this church has been stolen. You need look no further.' Pevsner described Great Paxton as the most advanced piece of architecture of its time in England; that at least cannot be stolen.

**Guyhirn:** Chapel.
About 3½ miles (5.5 km) north of March, over Guyhirn Bridge on the road to Wisbech St Mary, is this plain and comely building of

22

1660, originally a chapel of ease, now cared for by the Redundant Churches Fund. The interior is in marked contrast to the wealthy and elaborate churches hereabouts, simple, undecorated, wholly puritan.

**Harlton:** Assumption of the Blessed Virgin Mary.

Hidden away at the end of a lane, the church seems nothing special from the outside, but the interior is a real surprise. There is no clerestory, and one is immediately struck by the height and elegance of the arcades and the tower arch. Although the stone screen has lost its ornamentation, it is still impressive. Most of the building is fourteenth-century, but the large, impressive monument in the south aisle to Sir Henry Fryer, his parents and step-mother, dates from the 1630s. Notable also are the carvings of the apostles on the reredos in the style of Eric Gill, by H. J. Ellison, 1924. This is a cool and friendly church with much style; when it becomes too cool the ingenious heater, like a Victorian multi-faceted gas lamp, comes into action. Before leaving, look for the learned graffiti on the columns near the screen.

**Ickleton:** St Mary Magdalene.

This flint and pebble church, opposite the village green, has a remarkable interior. Much of the nave, including the columns of Barnack stone, is eleventh-century, as are the pillars in the crossing. Interesting features include a fine late fourteenth-century rood screen, oak pews from the late medieval period, a sixteenth-century pulpit, and especially the wall paintings which emerged during the cleaning of the church following a fire in 1979. The paintings show the Last Supper, the Betrayal, the Flagellation and Christ carrying the Cross, with various martyrdoms below. They are late twelfth-century but the bright colours and fine details have been lost. Above the chancel arch is a fourteenth-century painting of the Day of Judgement.

Outside is a fourteenth-century porch and a fine broach spire one hundred years older than the tower beneath it, with a sanctus bell. The village is close to the Icknield Way and has many fine old houses.

**Isleham:** St Andrew.

The richness of this church, dedicated in 1331, contrasts strongly with the austerity of the village. The expansive nave has a remarkably tall clerestory with uncommonly large windows; this, and the splendid roof adorned with angels bearing symbols of the Passion, was given by the Peyton family. An inscription around the roof asks for prayers for the family and ancestors of Crystofor Peyton 'qwych dyd mak thys rofe' in 1495. There are various memorials to the Peytons including two large six-poster tombs. Other features, among many, include a brass lectern dug out of the

*The Fryer memorial in Harlton church.*

*The nave roof at St Andrew's, Isleham, dates from 1495.*

fen in the nineteenth century and possibly made in the reign of Edward VI, several medieval bench-ends, a good early seventeenth-century communion rail and a fine south porch with a substantial late seventeenth-century door. Note the medieval lychgate. Nearby is the priory church of St Margaret of Antioch (see chapter 6).

**Kimbolton:** St Andrew.

This is a good symmetrical building with some thirteenth-century work. The local importance of the Montagus of Kimbolton Castle is reflected in the south chapel with several monuments and a large number of hatchments on display. The family vault is beneath the north chapel, entered by a Victorian Gothic doorway. The oak screen of the south chapel is fifteenth-century and has four paintings from about 1500 discovered beneath a coat of modern paint. This chapel also contains the unique Tiffany window, made in New York by Louis Comfort Tiffany for Consuelo, widow of the eighth Duke of Manchester, in memory of her twin daughters. Its mellow warmth and the portrayal of the figures are unlike anything in conventional English stained glass. Note also the very old font, rescued from use as a cattle trough in 1918. Outside, study the cornice of carvings at the top of the tower and admire the fine broach spire.

**Kingston:** All Saints and St Andrew.

Most of the church was rebuilt in 1488 following a fire. Once it glowed with wall paintings; today the one over the chancel is in quite good condition but the others have suffered as the result of Victorian restoration work on the building. Otherwise the interior is comparatively simple. There are some intriguing graffiti on the arcade columns and evidence of the fire in the south porch.

East of the church is the Old Rectory, a medieval house developed around an aisled timber hall of about 1300.

**Kirtling:** All Saints.

Tucked away behind the gatehouse of Kirtling Towers, this church with Norman and Perpendicular arches in the nave is light and spacious, if rather chilly. It is notable for several memorials to the North family, statesmen and soldiers who served the Tudors and Stuarts. The North Memorial Chapel made of local brick was built early in the sixteenth century and contains, among others, the elaborate six-poster tomb of the second Baron in full armour. There are fine old pews, including the Norths' box pews, and some splendid hatchments.

Beyond the churchyard is part of the square moat, wide and watered, that once surrounded Kirtling Towers. The Tudor mansion, visited by Queen Elizabeth I in 1578, has long disappeared; what remains is the gatehouse, privately occupied, and a Victorian replacement house.

**Leighton Bromswold: St Mary.**

A strong feeling of unity of composition gives the impression that the church was the work of a single architect, and this is partly accurate. By 1600 the thirteenth- to fifteenth-century building was in ruins. Rebuilding began in 1606 but funds ran out; then in 1626 George Herbert, the poet, became prebend and in the following years the rebuilding was completed with a complete re-roofing and re-furnishing. The tower was added by the Duke of Lennox in 1634. The chancel is essentially fourteenth-century and there are many fragments of the early building, but Herbert and various benefactors, including the Ferrars of nearby Little Gidding, achieved a wonderful harmony, strong and well proportioned, a cruciform church, aisleless, of uninterrupted space and light. A pulpit and identical reader's desk, both with sounding boards, stand either side of the chancel arch. The seating all dates from about 1626. Note the alabaster monuments in the north transept and the double piscina in the chancel. Outside there are good rainwater heads, some of them dated.

To the east of the churchyard is the gatehouse to what was intended to be Leighton Bromswold Castle, a projected rebuilding of an old manor house. It is an interesting and elaborate confection dating from 1616 and is now part of the Little Gidding community.

**Leverington: St Leonard.**

This large and splendid church reflects the prosperity of the silt fens on which it stands, good agricultural land reclaimed from the sea in the thirteenth century. The church has a fine tower topped by a 162 foot (49.4 metre) spire and a remarkable two-storey fourteenth-century porch. There are some exceptional windows including a Tree of Jesse window with 61 figures framed by the loops and scrolls of a vine, a good early font and a fifteenth-century wooden lectern. Tie-beams inserted in 1901 detract somewhat from the overall impression of the interior, but the church has much good and telling detail and is well cared for.

**Little Gidding: St John the Evangelist.**

This tiny church is one of the most famous in England. In 1626 Nicholas Ferrar, Member of Parliament and businessman, came to Little Gidding to found a religious community and was ordained deacon. Members of his family and their children formed the nucleus and the community soon grew to about forty members,

with a school and a few almspeople. They rebuilt a ruined medieval church and the chancel probably dates from that time. The community was based on prayer. Nicholas Ferrar wrote biblical concordances, which the members bound; they also cultivated the large gardens, wove tapestries and ran a medical dispensary. Many visitors came to Little Gidding, including King Charles I.

When Nicholas died in 1637 his brother John took over the leadership. During the Civil War Roundheads despoiled the church and threw the font and lectern into a pond; the lid of the font shows evidence of the damage. The community survived until 1657 when John and his sister Susanna both died and the other members disbanded. Nicholas's nephew inherited the estate; in 1714 he built the present nave and west front and restored the interior panelling. There was further restoration in 1853 when the stained glass windows and nave seating were installed as well as the fine brass chandelier.

Interest was redirected to Little Gidding in 1938 when a book by Alan Maycock on Ferrar and the community was published and T. S. Eliot wrote 'Little Gidding', the last and finest of his Four Quartets. Maycock's hope was that a community would return here and after the Second World War the Little Gidding fellowship was formed. The farmhouse was bought and gradually a new community came into being, known today as the Community of Christ the Sower, with a branch at Leighton Bromswold where Nicholas Ferrar's friend, the poet George Herbert, was once prebend.

With its beautiful panelling and gleaming brasswork the little church has a warm and welcoming feeling. It is a very special place 'where prayer has been valid', as Eliot wrote. Note the 1625 brass reredos, the medieval lectern, the brass font and hourglass stand. The tomb of Nicholas Ferrar is on the path leading to the west door. The church is usually open but if not you may enquire at the farmhouse.

**March: St Wendreda.**

The church is on the site of the original Saxon settlement, over a mile (1.6 km) from the centre of the town which developed around the old river Nene. The present St Wendreda's — a unique dedication, Wendreda a sister of Etheldreda, founder of Ely — dates mostly from the mid fourteenth and early fifteenth centuries. It is a handsome building with a 140 foot (42.5 metre) spire, a tall-windowed battlemented clerestory with intriguing designs between the windows on the outside, and beneath the tower an arch which once straddled the highway. Inside is one of the wonders of the county: the famous and fantastic angel roof. Of oak and double hammerbeam construction, it incorporates 118 carved angels in three tiers with wings widespread. Carved saints bearing symbols line the walls and almost hidden away is a figure of the devil. Clerestory and roof were installed together, the large windows providing light for the angels, who seem to move and ruffle their wings as you look up. A Norman font, a brass of 1517, an enormous Bible, a seventeenth-century gallery and, outside, a good collection of gargoyles and an attractive south porch are other features of this outstanding church.

**Peterborough:** Cathedral Church of St Peter, St Paul and St Andrew.

About AD 654 Peada, King of Mercia, founded a monastery at Medeshamstede, now Peterborough. The buildings were destroyed by the Danes, rebuilt and burnt down in 1116. Two years later another rebuilding was commenced by the abbot, John de Sais, and the new minster was consecrated in 1237. The nave, choir and great transept were completed first, followed by the west front in contrasting Early English style. There were various changes and additions in the fourteenth and fifteenth centuries and a major restoration in the 1880s. Peterborough became a cathedral in 1541.

The west front of Peterborough is one of the most striking in England with three enormous arches, 82 feet (25 metres) high. The porch was added more than a hundred years after the front was built, not always to the approval of experts in subsequent years. Inside there is an uninterrupted view along the strong and satisfying Norman nave to the altar over 450 feet (137 metres) away. The painted wooden nave ceiling dating from about 1220 is one of the earliest in Europe; the decoration is full of variety and vigour. The transepts also retain their original Norman ceilings, although the chancel ceiling dates from the fifteenth century. In the south wall of the choir steps lead down to the foundations of the Saxon church. One of the glories of the cathedral is the so-called New Building, the fifteenth-century retrochoir, with superb fan vaulting comparable with that at King's College Chapel in Cambridge.

Features of special interest in the cathedral include the Anglo-Saxon Monks' Stone, sometimes known as the Hedda Stone, in the retrochoir, the tomb of Catharine of Aragon in the north choir aisle and a very early oaken chest, fragments of medieval glass in the central apse window — the rest of the coloured glass is mediocre Victorian — and the memorial tablet near the west door to Robert Scarlett, sexton in the sixteenth century, who buried both Catharine of Aragon and Mary, Queen of Scots, whose body lay beneath the choir until moved to Westminster in 1612 by her son, James I.

Little is left of the various monastic buildings that once almost filled the south side of the precinct. The western gate, leading to the market place, was built by Abbot Benedict in the late twelfth century and inside to the north is the chancel of St Thomas's Chapel that once housed relics of Thomas à Becket brought here by the abbot from Canterbury where he was once prior. South of the gate is the King's Lodging, which incorporated the abbot's prison. The remains of the infirmary to the south of the chancel are worth visiting.

**Swaffham Prior:** St Mary, and St Cyriac and St Julitta.

The village is dominated by these two churches sharing the same elevated churchyard. The parish was divided about AD 1080 when the building of St Mary's began on the site of a Saxon church; nearly two hundred years later St Cyriac's was built for the second parish. In 1667 the parishes were united and St Cyriac's, apart from the tower, dating from 1493, was demolished. St Mary's, with its fine octagonal Norman tower and fifteenth-century arcades, remained the parish church until struck by lightning. It was considered too unsafe and unlucky to be used, and St Cyriac's was rebuilt in 1809-11 to take its place. Some eighty years later the situation was reversed; St Cyriac's was in such poor condition that restoration of St Mary's was put in hand. By 1906 St Mary's was again the parish church and St Cyriac's was left to decay. In 1976, however, it was restored as an amenity for the village.

**Thorney:** St Mary and St Botolph.

The religious foundation at Thorney dates from AD 662 when a small group of monks moved to the 'Isle of Thorns' to live as hermits. Their monastery was destroyed by the Danes in 870 but was re-founded in 972 for the Benedictine order, a portion of St Botolph's body being buried there. Developing into an abbey, Thorney's wealth and importance quickly increased. By 1108 new buildings were completed, including a splendid church five times the size of the present remnant, with six aisles and an enormous central tower. A range of monastic buildings and a chapter house were added later on the green south of the church. The Abbot of Thorney had a seat in the House of Lords.

After the Dissolution of the Monasteries most of the buildings were destroyed and the tower collapsed. The abbey lands were granted to the Earl of Bedford, who sent much of the building stone to various Cambridge colleges. However, in 1638 the remains of the church — the nave — were re-shaped and restored as the parish church; a new roof was

*Peterborough Cathedral.*

fitted and a smaller window inserted at the west end. The Norman arcades are now blind as the aisles were removed at that time. The present transepts were added in 1830. In 1980 there was a major restoration and the church is now in fine condition. With its twin towers and frieze of Anglo-Saxon saints the west front is one of the sights of Cambridgeshire and a poignant reminder of the former glory of Thorney.

**Trumpington: St Mary and St Nicholas.**

Beloved of brass-rubbers as it contains the second oldest brass in England, of Sir Roger de Trumpington (died 1289), this mostly fourteenth-century church has a rich and elaborately decorated interior, although it has been much restored both inside and out. The village itself, site of the bawdy happenings in Chaucer's 'Reeve's Tale', has been almost overwhelmed by Cambridge.

**Tydd St Giles: St Giles.**

The village is in the northern corner of the county with its sister, Tydd St Mary, just across the Lincolnshire border. St Giles's church consists of a nave with much twelfth- and thirteenth- century work and a separate tower, also thirteenth- century. It was original-ly a much larger building but the chancel was demolished in Gilbert Scott's restoration of 1868. The interior is trim and tidy with fine arcades and there is a good fourteenth-century west front. The church is a fascinating compendium of early architecture.

**Walsoken: All Saints.**

Walsoken is a suburb of Wisbech but the church lies just across the county boundary in Norfolk. Moreover, Pevsner described it as 'the grandest parish church in Norfolk', but its most likely visitors are those who have been first attracted to Wisbech, hence its inclusion here. It contains a good deal of fine Norman work, especially the arcades and the west door. The formidable tower is mostly Early English. Especially noteworthy are the carved roof, two fifteenth-century screens, the ornamented font of 1544, and wall paintings of Solomon and David. The interior — architecture, fittings, memorials — feels absolutely right. There are some excellent eighteenth-century headstones in the churchyard.

**Westley Waterless: St Mary the Less.**

This little church, whose tower collapsed in the 1850s, includes thirteenth- and fourteenth-century work but is chiefly notable for a superb pair of brasses made in 1325 to the memory of Sir John and Lady Alyne de Creke, the earliest known brasses of a married couple. Note also the fourteenth-century graffiti by a window in the south aisle recording the production of clusters from several vines, possibly grown by the church walls to provide wine for the mass. Waterless means water-leas, or

27

meadows; this is not a drought-stricken area though where the meadows were cannot be ascertained.

**Whittlesey:** St Mary.

The spire of St Mary's is the glory not only of Whittlesey but of the whole county. It was built in the mid fifteenth century with no expense spared, crowning a stately tower of impeccable proportions.

**Whittlesford:** St Andrew.

Tucked away along a lane and set in a well kept churchyard with bluebells in springtime, St Andrew's is one of Cambridgeshire's pleasantest churches. It has a Norman nave, crossing and central tower and a south aisle added in the thirteenth century. The timbered porch, now lurching over to one side, was donated by Henry Cyprian in the fifteenth century when various additions and alterations were made. Inside, among many delights, note a splendid iron chest of about 1400, fragments from an alabaster reredos encased in the north wall, well decorated Ten Commandments boards, traces of wall paintings, a thirteenth-century font and some good memorials. Outside, beneath the clock on the tower is a saucy carving known as a sheila-na-gig, probably of Celtic pagan origin; the details are just about distinguishable to the keenest eyesight but binoculars would be helpful.

**Willingham:** St Mary and All Saints.

An important and interesting church, it has many problems for the enthusiast to ponder. There are fragments of Saxon and Norman work, mostly in the porch, a fine fourteenth-century tower and spire, and an old sundial. Inside there is a wealth of wall painting including a splendid St Christopher (about 1380, restored in 1983), with fascinating detail and six fingers on his left hand, and a portrait of St Etheldreda by a window in the west wall. A beautifully painted screen of about 1320 is by the organ loft and there are two other well preserved early screens. One of the problems is the roof, double hammerbeam with angels. It looks as if it is compressed into a space rather too small for it and one theory is that it is a second-hand roof, originally in Barnwell Priory and moved to Willingham in 1613, the angels being added at a later date. The original purpose of the sacristy, early fourteenth-century, built wholly of stone and especially fine for a parish church, is also debatable; it may have been designed for use by the Bishops of Ely who were frequent visitors as they had estates nearby.

Thomas Hall is buried in the churchyard. When he died in 1747, aged five years and ten months, he had attained 'almost to the height and proportions of manhood'. By the age of

three he could throw a 17 pound (7.7 kg) blacksmith's hammer and he was already growing whiskers on his upper lip.

**Wisbech:** St Peter and St Paul.

This is a large town church with a semi-detached tower whose predecessor collapsed in late medieval times. The interior is at first confusing with a forest of pillars and no particular focal point. There are in effect two naves and two aisles, the result of fourteenth-century extensions. A grand James I royal arms, some old glass in the clerestory, a large brass of 1401 and two impressive seventeenth-century monuments are among other interesting features. The vestry at the south-east corner was built at the same time as the tower and is similarly elaborated; it was designed as a guild chapel.

Among other churches well worth visiting are Babraham, Bottisham, Cherry Hinton, Haslingfield, and Madingley, near Cambridge; Alconbury, Over and Fenstanton, near Huntingdon; Landwade and Snailwell, near Newmarket; and Conington, Glatton and Yaxley, near Peterborough. Several others are referred to in chapter 11.

**STAINED GLASS**

Although there is some good stained glass in the county, the most famous examples are in Cambridge itself — the wonderful sixteenth-century windows of King's College Chapel tell the story of the life of the Virgin Mary and of Jesus, together with the Old Testament foreshadowings. Peterhouse has a seventeenth-century Crucifixion window and others by Burne-Jones. In Trinity Library is a remarkable eighteenth-century window commemorating Isaac Newton, while Jesus College Chapel and All Saints' Church close by have good windows by Morris and Company, some designed by Burne-Jones and Ford Madox Brown. Ely Cathedral has a large collection of Victorian glass and the Stained Glass Museum (see chapter 7), while Peterborough Cathedral also has much Victorian glass.

Near Cambridge, Babraham has a fine east window by John Piper and there are many fragments of old glass in Madingley church. There are examples of fourteenth-century heraldic glass in St Andrew's, Wimpole, and of fifteenth-century saints and apostles in St Nicholas's, Landwade. To the west, there is the rare Tiffany window in St Andrew's, Kimbolton. In the north of the county, Wisbech St Mary has some medieval continental glass and in Thorney Abbey the Passion is illustrated in six panels of fifteenth-century glass from Cologne. One of the best and most intriguing windows is in St Leonard's, Leverington (see above).

*Anglesey Abbey, converted to a private house after the Dissolution, has been much altered in the twentieth century.*

# 6
# Historic buildings and gardens

**Anglesey Abbey,** Lode, Cambridge. Telephone: 0223 811200. National Trust.

Originally a priory founded in the twelfth century, the present building incorporates the undercroft and part of the prior's lodging. It became a private house after the Dissolution of the Monasteries and was much altered and extended in succeeding centuries. Among its owners were Thomas Hobson (of 'Hobson's choice'), Sir George Downing (of Downing College and Downing Street) and the local historian Edward Hailstone. In 1926 the abbey was bought by Lord Fairhaven who spent forty years remodelling the house and garden and made it a home for his extensive collections of furniture, paintings and works of art. One room is devoted to paintings of Windsor Castle and there are collections of mosaics, tapestries, crucifixes, gemstones and clocks, all beautifully displayed.

The splendid 100-acre (40 ha) garden, with rare trees, avenues, vistas, lawns and superb floral displays in spring and summer, has many exceptional examples of statuary and is one of the finest gardens open to the public anywhere. Lode watermill (chapter 8) is on the edge of the estate.

**Burghley House,** Stamford PE9 3JY. Telephone: 0780 52451.

The county boundary runs through the park but the administrators consider the house itself to be in Lincolnshire.

**Denny Abbey,** Waterbeach. Telephone: 022024 489. English Heritage. Access to the abbey is 2 miles (3.2 km) north of Waterbeach on the A10.

This is a complicated building with an involved history and either a guide or a guidebook is needed to make full sense of it. In 1160 a group of monks from Ely moved here and built a church. A few years later the property was granted to the Knights Templar, who extended the buildings and used them as an infirmary. In 1308 the Templars were suppressed and about thirty years later the Countess of Pembroke took over and enlarged the buildings to accommodate the nuns of St Clare (the Poor Clares), who moved in from their own small abbey in Waterbeach. Lady Pembroke became the abbess and added lodgings for herself as well as a large new church, refectory and cloister. Much of this was destroyed after the Dissolution and in later years most of the remaining buildings were absorbed in a grand farmhouse. Careful study of the surviving buildings reveals details of their history with many blocked doors and windows and the outlines of what was once here. There are some impressive Norman remains.

**Docwra's Manor,** Shepreth. Telephone: 0763 61473.

Originally a sixteenth-century manor, the house was extensively rebuilt in the 1740s. The varied and attractive gardens are open to the public on certain Sundays between April and October, or by appointment.

**Duxford Chapel,** Duxford. English Heritage. Key from the Red Lion Inn.

The chapel belonged to St John's Hospital and was built in the early thirteenth century. In the early fifteenth century it was largely rebuilt to become a chantry with the duty of collecting alms at Whittlesford Bridge. Later it was used as a barn attached to the Red Lion, but has now been carefully restored.

**Elton Hall,** near Peterborough PE8 6SH. Telephone: 08324 468.

The hall has been the home of the Proby family for over three hundred years. The land was granted to Sir Peter Proby, Lord Mayor of London, by Elizabeth I and much of the present building, incorporating the medieval chapel and gatehouse, was completed by Sir Thomas Proby in 1666. Extensive alterations and enlargements took place in succeeding centuries, resulting in the fascinating mixture of styles seen today. Especially notable rooms are the state drawing room, the inner library and the dining room with its fine collection of paintings. The hall contains much good furniture. The gardens include a Victorian rose garden with nearly a thousand roses.

**Hinchingbrooke House,** Huntingdon. Telephone: 0480 51121.

Originally a Benedictine nunnery, Hinchingbrooke House was much extended and developed by Sir Henry Cromwell in the Elizabethan era. The gatehouse was removed here from Ramsey Abbey. It was sold to the Montagu family in 1627 and remained in their ownership until 1960. Now it is owned by the County Council and houses the Sixth Form Centre of Hinchingbrooke School and a museum (see chapter 7). It is a handsome house with well proportioned rooms.

**Island Hall,** Post Street, Godmanchester, Huntingdon. Telephone: 0480 59676.

This fine eighteenth-century family house has identical front and rear elevations and fine panelled rooms. In the gardens next to the river the older of Godmanchester's two 'Chinese' bridges used to stand. It collapsed some years ago but is now being rebuilt. The house is still a family home.

**Isleham Priory,** Isleham. English Heritage. Key from 10 Sun Street.

The priory church of St Margaret of Antioch dates from about 1100. The priory was an offshoot of a Benedictine abbey in Brittany and owned 100 acres (40.5 ha) of land with a few monks in residence. It was suppressed in 1414 and from 1450 the building belonged to Pembroke College. In later years it was used as a barn, hence the massive doorway made to accommodate farm carts. The interior, consisting of nave, chancel and sanctuary, is simple and undecorated. Outside note the herringbone brickwork and, in the meadow behind, the outline of fishponds that once supplied the monks of Ely. The house opposite was also part of the priory at one time.

**Kimbolton Castle,** Kimbolton. Open on bank holidays and summer Sunday afternoons.

Sir John Vanbrugh was the architect of the present Kimbolton Castle, completed by 1714 for the fourth Earl of Manchester. There had been at least three previous buildings on the site but only a few traces of the latest of these remain. It is a solid, formal building, rather heavy in style, impressive rather than elegant. Inside, however, are superb painted ceilings by the Venetian artist Pellegrini, most notably above the staircase and in the Boudoir. Pellegrini also painted the walls and altar surround in the chapel. The gatehouse was designed by Robert Adam and built about 1765. The building now houses Kimbolton School.

**Leper Chapel,** St Mary Magdalene, Barnwell Bridge, Cambridge. Cambridge Preservation Society. Key from the house nearby.

This Norman chapel was once the chapel of a leper hospital at Stourbridge and is of much architectural interest and importance. In its time it has served as a storehouse for Stourbridge Fair and as a stable.

**Longthorpe Tower,** Peterborough. Telephone: 0733 268482. 2 miles (3.2 km) west of Peterborough on the A47.

The tower is a square construction with walls nearly seven feet (2 metres) thick. It was built in about 1300 as an addition to an even older hall. A remarkable series of wall paintings has been discovered in the principal room. They include illustrations of biblical scenes, moralities, symbolic representations and pictures of flowers and birds. They date from about 1330 and are painted in the style of old illustrated manuscripts.

**Peckover House,** Wisbech. Telephone: 0945 583463. National Trust.

This outstanding town house was built in 1722 and was given to the National Trust in 1943. It was originally known as Bank House and was bought in about 1800 by Jonathan Peckover, who opened his bank in a wing since pulled down. The interior is notable for the excellent woodwork and plasterwork decoration, seen at its best in the drawing room. The library and adjoining wing were added in 1878. The contents of the house come from a

*Wimpole Hall dates mostly from the eighteenth century.*

number of sources as it was empty when handed to the Trust. There is much good eighteenth-century furniture, the Cornwallis Collection of portraits, portraits of members of the Peckover family, many of them major benefactors of Wisbech, and several paintings and prints of local interest. The garden is a model of the gardener's art with a wonderful variety of trees, shrubs and flowers and an orangery with orange trees said to be three hundred years old. There is an eighteenth-century stable block in the grounds.

14 and 19 North Brink are also owned by the National Trust and are privately occupied. To the north 48 acres (19.5 ha) of land given to the Trust with the house by the Honourable Alexandrina Peckover and an additional 18 acres (7.3 ha) obtained later are leased for playing fields and cultivation.

**Thorpe Hall,** Peterborough. Open from time to time; enquiries to Tourist Information, Town Hall, Peterborough. Telephone: 0733 63141.

The hall is 1½ miles (2.4 km) west of Peterborough on the south side of the A47. It was built from 1653 to 1656 by Peter Mills, an important London architect, for the Lord Chief Justice, Oliver St John. It is a substantial square-set building, beautifully proportioned and a leading example of the architectural style of its time. For some years the hall was used as a hospital annex until it was taken over

in 1974 by the Peterborough Development Corporation. A full restoration of the interior is planned and eventually it will become a cultural and leisure centre.

**Wimpole Hall,** Wimpole. Telephone: 0223 207257. National Trust. 8 miles (13 km) south-west of Cambridge on A603.

Set in a 350 acre (142 ha) park, Wimpole is by far the largest house in the county. The first house on the site was built between 1640 and 1670 but nearly all of the present building dates from the eighteenth century. James Gibbs, Henry Flitcroft and Sir John Soane were the architects responsible for the design and development of the buildings, and Charles Bridgeman, 'Capability' Brown and Humphry Repton were among those who extended and improved the gardens and park. From 1740 to 1894 the estate was owned by the Earls of Hardwicke. In the following years it fell into a dilapidated condition and most of the contents were sold. Then in 1938 Wimpole was bought by Captain George Bambridge, whose wife, Elsie, was the daughter of Rudyard Kipling. Captain Bambridge died in 1943 but his widow continued the restoration he had begun and gradually filled the rooms with suitable furniture and pictures. She died in 1976, leaving the house and estate to the National Trust.

Among the glories of Wimpole are Soane's Yellow Drawing Room, Gibbs's library, and the chapel, designed by Gibbs and elaborately

*The sham ruin of 1768 in the park of Wimpole Hall.*

decorated by Thornhill. The park contains a ruined Gothic tower built in 1768 as a landscape feature, lakes and a 'Chinese' bridge. The great 2¼ mile (3.6 km) South Avenue, ruined by Dutch elm disease, has been replanted with limes by the Trust.

**Wimpole Home Farm,** Wimpole. Telephone: 0223 207257. National Trust.

Dating from 1794, the Home Farm has been restored by the National Trust and houses a variety of rare breeds of livestock that were common in the eighteenth and nineteenth centuries. The 150 foot (46 metre) long Great Barn is now a museum of farm machinery and implements. There is an area where children may view the smaller animals and a woodland area nearby. Refreshments are available at the hall and the farm and there is a picnic area by the main car park.

Cobb's Wood farm walk (2 miles, 3.2 km) begins opposite the entrance to Wimpole Home Farm. It provides a tour of a modern working farm, with information boards explaining what is growing in each field and the purposes of the various buildings and enclosures.

The parish church of St Andrew is a few yards from the Hall. Originally it was the centre of the village of Wimpole that was demolished when the park and gardens were enclosed in the late seventeenth century. Much of the church was rebuilt in 1749 by Henry Flitcroft but alterations in 1887 changed its character. The fourteenth-century north chapel contains a fine collection of monuments to members of the Yorke (Hardwicke) family.

The village of New Wimpole is a row of houses by the edge of the park on the Cambridge road.

# 7
# Museums and art galleries

Opening hours are variable and it is advisable to check in advance before making a special journey.

## CAMBRIDGE
**Cambridge and County Folk Museum,** 2/3 Castle Street, Cambridge CB3 0AQ. Telephone: 0223 355159.

The sixteenth-century building housing the museum used to be the White Horse Inn and one of the exhibits is the bar of the inn as it was before closure in 1934. Into eleven rooms is packed an extraordinary assortment of items illustrating the domestic, trading and rural life of the past three hundred years. One room is devoted to fenland life with a reconstruction of a fenland kitchen. Other rooms contain toys and games, nineteenth- and early twentieth-century kitchen equipment, tools and gear of a large number of trades and crafts, and objects relating to university life and to the city in general. A room is reserved for special exhibitions.

**Cambridge Darkroom,** Dales Brewery, Gwydir Street, Cambridge. Telephone: 0223 350725.

Opened in 1984, the Darkroom is internationally known for its exhibition and workshop programme. Major displays of contemporary photography are mounted regularly, with associated talks and lectures.

**Fitzwilliam Museum,** Trumpington Street, Cambridge CB2 1RB. Telephone: 0223 332900.

The Fitzwilliam is a museum of international importance. It was founded by Viscount Fitzwilliam, who left his own extensive collection to the university with funds for an appropriate building. Building began in 1837, to designs by George Basevi, and the museum was opened to the public in 1848, although the entrance hall was not completed until the 1870s. Late twentieth-century additions have made the Fitzwilliam one of the most splendid museum buildings in England.

The Fitzwilliam holds outstanding collections of antiquities from Greece, Rome and the Near East, and of coins, medals, ceramics (English, European and Far Eastern), European and Oriental fans and armour. There is a wide-ranging manuscript collection and autograph scores by many great composers. The upper floor houses a superb display of paintings representing all schools and periods of European art and some fine furniture and clocks. There are special exhibitions of major importance throughout the year and a well

stocked museum shop.

**Gallery on the Cam,** Jesus Lock, near Chesterton Road, Cambridge.

A converted barge houses exhibitions in a variety of media throughout the year.

**Heffer's,** Sidney Street, Cambridge.

Regular exhibitions, mostly of contemporary work by local artists, are held on the top floor of the shop.

**Kettle's Yard,** Castle Street, Cambridge CB3 0AQ. Telephone: 0223 352124.

Kettle's Yard consists of a house with a gallery attached. The house, developed from four old cottages, belonged to Jim Ede, who left his collection of paintings, sculpture, furniture, books and other items to the university in 1966. The house was extended and the gallery added in 1970.

Larger than it looks from outside, the house is carefully arranged as a private home; everything is accessible and nothing is labelled. There is a large number of paintings by the primitive Cornish marine artist Alfred Wallis, a room full of drawings by Henri Gaudier-Brzeska, and works by Henry Moore, Ben Nicholson, Naum Gabo, Brancusi, Joan Miro, and others. There are fine pieces of eighteenth-century furniture, oriental carpets, collections of stones and shells, all representing one man's taste and all friendly and informal. The gallery mounts exhibitions during the year of contemporary or recent work in painting, sculpture, mixed media and photography. There is an accompanying education programme of lectures and workshops.

**Museum of Archaeology and Anthropology,** Downing Street, Cambridge CB2 3DZ. Telephone: 0223 337733.

Closely associated, like the other university museums, with academic research, the museum is part of the Faculty of 'Arch and Anth'. The Gallery of World Prehistory and Local Archaeology was completely renewed in 1984 on the occasion of the museum's centenary. The anthropological displays are closed for refurbishment and will be reopened in 1989/90.

**Museum of Classical Archaeology,** Sidgwick Avenue, Cambridge CB3 9DA. Telephone: 0223 335153.

The main attraction here is the comprehensive collection of plaster casts of Greek and Roman sculpture.

**Museum of Technology,** Riverside, Cambridge CB5 8HN. Enquiries to the Honorary Secretary.

The museum building is a preserved Victorian pumping station and houses steam, gas and electrically powered pumping engines and other items of historic industrial interest, including a printing shop. On holiday weekends the unique Hathorn Davey pumping engines may be in steam.

**Museum of Zoology,** Downing Street, Cambridge CB2 3EJ. Telephone: 0223 336650.

A wide-ranging collection of animal, bird, insect and invertebrate life is housed here, together with fossil specimens of extinct animals.

**Scott Polar Research Institute,** Lensfield Road, Cambridge CB2 1ER. Telephone: 0223 336540.

Exhibits at this small public museum are drawn from a rich collection of polar material with special displays illustrating different polar expeditions, wildlife, ethnic arts and crafts, scientific research and other topics. There are extensive holdings of manuscripts, watercolours, drawings and photographs, with many personal relics of the great explorers. The letters, notes and personal possessions of the members of Scott's final expedition, 1910-12, are especially moving, and Edward Wilson's paintings of Antarctica are remarkable.

**Sedgwick Museum,** Downing Street, Cambridge CB2 3EQ. Telephone: 0223 355463.

The special attraction is the vast collection of fossils including mounted skeletons of a dinosaur and other animals. Rocks and building and ornamental stones of the widest variety are also on display. The Sedgwick connects with the **Mineralogical Museum,** which holds extensive collections of British and foreign minerals.

**Whipple Museum of the History of Science,** Free School Lane, Cambridge. Telephone: 0223 334540.

Early scientific instruments and equipment used across the whole range of the sciences are on display and there are regular programmes of special exhibitions. The museum is housed in the seventeenth-century Free School building, close to the old Cavendish Laboratories — perhaps the most famous laboratories in the whole history of science.

**CHATTERIS**
**Chatteris Museum,** Grove House, High Street, Chatteris. Telephone: 03543 2414.

A small museum housed in the Fenland District Offices, it has displays of early flint implements and pottery, fossils, Roman jewel-lery and natural history. There is a Victoriana room and collections of tools and equipment used in local trades and agriculture; also a set of eighteenth-century mobile stocks.

**DUXFORD**
**Imperial War Museum,** Duxford Airfield, Duxford, Cambridge CB2 4QR. Telephone: .0223 833963. Access is easy from the M11/A505 junction (exit 10).

Duxford was a famous Fighter Command station during the Battle of Britain and the airfield now houses a branch of the Imperial War Museum. The exhibits include nearly one hundred historic aircraft, with many examples from both world wars, and the Duxford Aviation Society's collection of civil aircraft, including Concorde 01. On site are tanks and other military vehicles, submarines, artillery and special exhibitions. You may watch historic aircraft being restored in some of the hangars. Other attractions include the Astra cinema, in 1940s style (open on Sundays in the summer), a children's adventure playground and a licensed restaurant. On many Sundays during the year there are flying displays, including aerobatics, and other events such as military vehicle and fire engine rallies. In summer pleasure flights are available.

**ELY**
**Ely Museum,** Sacrist's Gate, High Street, Ely. Telephone: 0353 2311.

The museum specialises in objects of local historical and archaeological importance and also holds collections of local agricultural implements, fenland tools, toys and photographs. The museum will reopen in late 1988 after undergoing major structural repairs.

**Stained Glass Museum,** Ely Cathedral, Ely. Telephone: 0223 60148 or 0353 5103.

The museum was opened in 1979 in the north triforium of Ely Cathedral. On display is a wide-ranging collection of examples of stained glass from the fourteenth century to the present day from all over Britain. The eighteenth-century pictorial tradition, the Gothic revival, the late Victorian period, including Burne-Jones, the early twentieth century and Scottish glass are all well represented. There are scale models of a contemporary stained glass workshop showing the processes of designing and constructing a window. The visitor may also enjoy views of the cathedral from an unusual angle.

**HADDENHAM**
**The Farmland Museum,** 50 High Street, Haddenham CB6 3XB. Telephone: 0353 740381.

Originating from a schoolboy's enthusiastic collecting instinct, the Farmland Museum now owns nearly a hundred items of horse-drawn

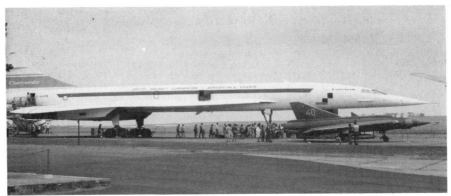

*Concorde 01 is one of many historic aircraft at the Imperial War Museum, Duxford.*

farming equipment and a good range of local domestic items of the nineteenth century. There are blacksmith's and wheelwright's shops and displays relating to natural history, geology, archaeology and rural crafts.

## HISTON
**The Histon Gallery,** 11 High Street, Histon. Telephone: 022023 4871.

There are regular shows here of paintings and sculpture by recognised artists from Britain and overseas.

## HUNTINGDON
**Cromwell Museum,** Grammar School Walk, Huntingdon. Telephone: 0480 425830.

The museum is housed in what survives of the old grammar school once attended by Oliver Cromwell. The building was originally part of the Hospital of St John and dates from the twelfth century. It contains portraits and other exhibits relating to Cromwell and his family and to the Parliament and Commonwealth (1640-60).

**Hinchingbrooke House,** Hinchingbrooke School, Huntingdon PE18 6BN. Telephone: 0480 51121.

The museum is controlled by the school governors. It contains portraits and various relics of the Cromwell and Montagu families and a large collection of Huntingdonshire maps. There are also relics of the nunnery which once occupied the site. (See also chapter 6.)

## MARCH
**March and District Museum,** High Street, March PE15 9JJ. Telephone: 0354 55300.

The collection of this folk museum concentrates on the locality with domestic, trade and agricultural exhibits and photographs and documents relating to March, its people and history, and the surrounding fenland. Outside there is a reconstructed nineteenth-century forge and fenland cottage. Local artists and craftsmen hold occasional displays.

## PETERBOROUGH
**Lady Lodge Arts Centre,** Goldhay Way, Orton Goldhay, Peterborough PE2 0JQ. Telephone: 0733 237073.

The lively programme of arts events and activities here includes children's shows, family days, play schemes, jazz and folk concerts and theatre, with local, regional and national exhibitions. Classes, weekend workshops, community projects and courses are available.

**Peterborough City Museum and Art Gallery,** Priestgate, Peterborough. Telephone: 0733 43329.

A handsome building houses several well lit and informative displays. An archaeological gallery tells the story of the district from prehistoric through Roman to Anglo-Saxon times. In contrast there are carefully set-out Victorian living rooms and bedrooms and a well stocked general store. In another gallery is a unique display of intricately worked models made of bone, straw and wood by French prisoners-of-war held at Norman Cross during the Napoleonic Wars. Local history, industry and militaria are also represented as well as ceramics, glass and domestic items. The art gallery has a permanent collection and emphasises contemporary work in its special exhibitions. The museum holds a large collection of John Clare manuscripts.

## RAMSEY
**Ramsey Rural Museum,** The Woodyard, Ramsey. Telephone: 0487 813223.

This small museum displays agricultural implements and machinery and local bygones.

## ST IVES

**Norris Museum,** The Broadway, St Ives. Telephone: 0480 65101.

The riverside building contains a fascinating exhibition of fen skating as well as bone and straw work by French prisoners-of-war. There is a good archaeological collection and many items relating to the history of Huntingdonshire. A research library is attached to the museum. Outside are two stone Roman coffins and the judgement seat of the court of the Hundred of Hurstingstone, known as the 'Abbot's Chair'.

## ST NEOTS

**Longsands Museum,** Longsands Community College, St Neots PE19 1LQ. Telephone: 0480 72229 extension 48.

The museum is housed in the college and is used by local schools as a teaching resource but is open to the public by appointment. It holds a large and important collection of Romano-British votive figures as well as a number of archaeological items and exhibits illustrating local crafts, trades and agriculture and the history of the area from earliest times.

## TRUMPINGTON

**Trumpington Gallery,** Trumpington Road, Trumpington, Cambridge.

In this converted cottage exhibitions in a variety of media are held throughout the year.

## WHITTLESEY

**Whittlesey Museum,** Market Street, Whittlesey. Telephone: 0733 202276.

The museum is in the Town Hall and displays exhibits relating to the history of the area, featuring brickyards, railways, fen drainage, sports and pastimes as well as industries, business and agriculture. An Elizabethan herb garden is among the outdoor exhibits.

## WISBECH

**Wisbech and Fenland Museum,** Museum Square, Wisbech PE13 1ES. Telephone: 0945 583817.

The museum, purpose-built by J. C. Buckler in 1847, stands close to the church and the mansion on the site of Wisbech Castle. As well as an extensive archaeological collection, much of it local, there are displays of ceramics, including Staffordshire figures, stuffed birds, items illustrating fenland activities including the manufacture of woad, and much about Wisbech history. The collection of Thomas Clarkson, the opponent of the slave trade, is housed here. A large showcase contains shop fittings and contents, with advertising material, from the early twentieth century, all removed from a shop in Elm on its closure. The library, accessible by appointment, contains eleven thousand volumes and much important autograph and manuscript material.

*The chapel, mall and great wall at the American Military Cemetery, Coton, near Cambridge.*

# 8
# Other places to visit

**American Military Cemetery and Memorial,** Coton. 3 miles (4.8 km) west of Cambridge on A1303.

This is the only Second World War American military cemetery in Britain. It was dedicated in 1956 and covers 30½ acres (12.3 ha). Buried here are 3811 American war dead, many of them members of the US Air Force who flew from bases in East Anglia. Commemorated also are 5125 of the missing, whose names are inscribed on the great wall, 472 feet (144 metres) in length, on the south side of the mall which extends from the flagpole to the memorial chapel. Along the length of the mall is a series of reflecting ponds with rose gardens on either side and to the north are the graves arranged in quarter concentric arcs. The chapel includes the museum chamber dominated by a vast map illustrating the Atlantic sea routes and the air assault on occupied Europe. A mosaic ceiling by an American artist, Francis Scott Bradford, extends over the museum chamber and the smaller devotional chapel. It commemorates the dead of the United States Army Air Force and shows a fleet of ghostly aircraft making their last flight, accompanied by mourning angels. The grounds of the cemetery are planted with ornamental trees and shrubs and there is a visitors' information centre.

**Cambridge Medieval Brassrubbing Centre,** St Giles Church, Castle Hill, Cambridge. Telephone: 0223 835055.

There are ninety facsimile brasses to choose from and materials are provided.

**Chilford Hundred Vineyard,** Balsham Road, Linton CB1 6LE. Telephone: 0223 892641.

This is the county's largest vineyard. There are regular conducted tours and wine tastings and in Chilford Barns there are a screen printing press and an art gallery.

**Ferry Meadows Country Park,** Peterborough. Telephone: 0733 234443. Vehicle access is off the A605 about 4 miles (6.5 km) west of Peterborough city centre.

This 500 acre (202 ha) country park is the recreational centre of the larger Nene Park, the riverside area between Peterborough and Wansford. It was opened in 1978. There is ample free car parking, a visitors' centre and shop, children's play areas equipped with climbing frames and slides, and cafés. Two large lakes are available for water sports (telephone: 0733 234418) including sailing, board sailing, angling and model boating, while the *Nene Star* gives river cruising trips.

Caravan and camping sites are provided (telephone: 0733 233526). There are a bird reserve with hides, horse riding, pony and trap rides and a miniature railway. Two eighteen-hole golf courses and a pitch and putt course are open to everyone. There are miles of footpaths and cycleways throughout the Meadows and the Nene Park, and the Nene Valley Steam Railway runs through with stations near the entrance to the Meadows and at Orton nearer Peterborough (see below). Facilities for disabled people are a feature. Various special events take place in the summer season.

**Grafham Water,** West Perry. Anglian Water (Recreation and Conservation Officer), Chivers Way, Histon, Cambridge CB4 4ZY. Telephone: 0223 235235. Approach by B661, 2 miles (3 km) west of junction with A1 at Buckden.

This attractively landscaped reservoir with a 2¼ square mile (6.5 sq km) surface area is an active recreation centre open to the public. Activities include trout fishing and sailing (launch facilities are available for day sailing). There is a nature reserve with waymarked paths, nature trails and birdwatching hides. Facilities for the disabled include wheelchair access to one of the hides, toilets and a fishing boat which can be used by those in wheelchairs. A comfortable residential centre is home to a variety of courses throughout the year. Car parking at Grafham is free and there is also a caravan park.

**Hilton Maze,** Hilton, near Godmanchester.

Hilton is a small village 3 miles (5 km) south-east of Godmanchester, accessible from the A14 and A604. The maze is by the eastern edge of the village next to the large green. According to the obelisk in the centre it was cut in 1660 by William Sparrow, who lived in a nearby house now demolished. It is a small turf maze, one of only eight surviving in England, and is scheduled as an ancient monument. Such mazes are reputed to have been used in fertility rites and for casting out the devil, who was said to be able to travel only in a straight line. Close by is a tree planted in memory of the famous landscape gardener 'Capability' Brown, once lord of the manor here, who 'planted a million others'.

**Hobson's Conduit,** Cambridge. On the corner of Lensfield Road and Trumpington Road.

The handsome elaborate hexagonal Jacobean fountain here is fed by Hobson's Conduit, an artificial river that flows past the Botanic Gardens parallel to Trumpington

Road. The fountain and river were completed in 1614 and supplied the town with water from springs at Nine Wells, 3 miles (4.8 km) to the south. A memorial obelisk stands by the Nine Wells recording the names of those responsible for the scheme, including Thomas Hobson, the famous university carrier of 'Hobson's choice', for whom a supply of water to his extensive stables was extremely valuable. The fountain was moved from the Market Place to this site in 1856 and was replaced by the present inelegant construction. Water from the conduit flows alongside Trumpington Road to flush out the gutters and also supplies the bathing pools in Christ's and Emmanuel colleges.

**Landbeach Marina Park,** Ely Road, Waterbeach. Telephone: 0223 860019.

This leisure park has ample facilities for camping and caravanning and is centred on a series of lakes. Sailing, boating and angling are among the principal attractions.

**Linton Zoo,** Linton. Telephone: 0223 891308. On B1052, off A604, 9 miles (14.5 km) south-east of Cambridge.

In a landscaped setting of over 10 acres (4 ha) the zoo incorporates a wildlife breeding centre. Lions, leopards, pumas, panthers, bears, binturongs, llamas and a wide variety of birds, insects and reptiles are on view. There is

a cafeteria and several picnic areas. Access for prams, push-chairs and wheelchairs presents no problems.

**Mepal Outdoor Centre,** Chatteris Road, Mepal. Telephone: 03543 2251.

Water sports are the speciality of this centre which has many facilities for use by disabled people and safe play areas for younger children.

**Nene Valley Railway,** Wansford Station, Stibbington, Peterborough PE8 6LR. Telephone: 0780 782854 or 782921 (talking timetable).

Opened in 1845, the Nene Valley line was closed by British Rail in 1972. Shortly afterwards the Peterborough Railway Society took over the line and within a few years had rebuilt it almost completely. It is now open for 7½ miles (12 km) from Wansford to Peterborough, with an extension to Yarwell Mill west of Wansford station. The railway is unique as it uses continental engines and rolling stock as well as British. Among the locomotives are a French Nord 4-6-0, Swedish and Danish tank engines, a German tank engine, *92 Squadron* from the old Southern Railway, *Britannia* and *City of Peterborough* from British Rail, and 'Thomas the Tank Engine'. Timetabled services run during the summer with special 'Santa' trains in December, nearly all of them steam-hauled. Wansford station has extensive

*Hilton Maze was cut in 1660.*

*'Thomas the Tank Engine' at the Nene Valley Railway.*

workshops as well as a shop, refreshments, exhibition and a bar. Timetables and full information about the attractive route and the history and resources of the railway are available from the station.

**Prickwillow Engine,** Prickwillow, near Ely (OS 143: TL 598825).

The engine house was built in 1880 for a beam engine, superseded in 1923 by a five-cylinder Mirrlees, Bickerton and Day diesel engine driving an Appold type centrifugal pump. A modern diesel engine and pump were installed in 1974 and when the 'Mirrlees' was retired in 1982 the Prickwillow Engine Trust was formed to 'maintain, improve and operate' it. The 'Mirrlees' is started, by compressed air, on certain days during the summer.

**Stretham Old Engine,** Stretham, near Ely (OS 153: TL 515739).

Built in 1831 at a cost of about £5000 the Stretham engine was installed to help drain the Waterbeach Level of the fenland. Originally it had two boilers and a third was added in 1847; all three were replaced in the 1870s. Other alterations and improvements were made in the following years, including a new scoop-wheel with a diameter of 37 feet (11.3 metres) able to lift 30 tons of water on each revolution — about 120 tons a minute. The engine worked on average for about 770 hours a year, with the longest period of non-stop working in 1919 when it ran for 47 days and nights after a bank had given way. A diesel engine was installed in 1925 and was last used in March 1941. The Stretham engine is the only survivor in good condition of the 41 steam engines built in the fens between 1818 and 1852. Although it is no longer in full working order all the essential components are there. It is open to visitors throughout the year and can be closely inspected on all levels.

**University Botanic Garden,** Bateman Street, Cambridge. Telephone: 0223 336265.

There are three entrances to the gardens, in Bateman Street, Trumpington Street and Hills Road. The gardens were established on this 20 acre (8 ha) site in 1846 when they were moved from Free School Lane. The iron gates of the old gardens are at the Trumpington Street entrance. The gardens have a rich variety of trees, bushes, shrubs and plants and several greenhouses and are primarily a research facility, but they are open to the public on weekdays and summer Sundays.

## WINDMILLS AND WATERMILLS

**Barnack,** near Stamford. Telephone: 0780 52075.

The tower mill on a minor road one mile (1.6 km) west of the village is open at weekends.

**Bourn,** near Cambridge. Telephone: 0223 243830.

On the minor road between Bourn and Caxton this weatherboarded post mill dates from 1636 and is among the oldest in England. It has been restored to working order by the Cambridge Preservation Society.

**Fulbourn,** near Cambridge.

Built in 1808, this smock mill stands on a hill at the western end of the village. It has been restored and is open at certain times — see the notice on the gate.

**Great Chishill,** near Royston. Telephone: 0763 838545.

A restored open-trestle mill lies on the west side of the village.

**Great Gransden,** near St Neots. Information from Cambridgeshire County Property Department. Telephone: 0223 317323.

This post mill dates from 1674 and has good machinery. The key is obtainable in the village (see the notice at the mill).

**Houghton,** near St Ives. Telephone: 0480 301494. National Trust.

The first watermill on this site by the Great Ouse was built about AD 970 and is recorded in Doomsday Book. The present building is of the seventeenth and eighteenth centuries and was working until 1930. Some of the machinery has been restored and is in action at certain times. The mill is an exceptionally handsome building in a picturesque setting.

**Lode,** Anglesey Abbey, Lode. Telephone: 0223 811200. National Trust.

The eighteenth-century watermill worked until 1910 and is now restored to working order and open at weekends. Operated by Quy Water, the mill can be seen at work on the first Sunday of the month from Easter to October and visitors may buy the flour.

**Maxey,** near Market Deeping. Telephone: 0778 343191.

This watermill on the river Welland dates from 1779 and produces pig food.

**Over,** near St Ives. Telephone: 0954 30742.

A mid Victorian tower mill to the south of the village is now restored to working order. It is open daily for the sale of flour, but telephone for full access.

**Sacrewell Mill and Country Life Centre,** near Peterborough. Telephone: 0780 782222. North of A47 on east side of junction with A1.

An eighteenth-century watermill, in working order, is part of a farm and country life centre administered by the William Scott Abbott Charitable Trust. There are displays of country crafts and skills, agricultural tools and machinery and other items connected with country life.

**Soham,** near Ely. Telephone: 0353 707625.

Downfield Mill is a tower mill dating from 1726 and restored to full working order with flour on sale throughout the year. It is open to the public on Sundays and bank holidays. For visits at other times telephone or enquire at 23 Military Road, Soham.

**Wicken Fen.** Telephone: 0353 720274. National Trust.

This drainage mill or wind pump was removed to this site in the National Trust reserve from Adventurers' Fen (see chapter 2). It is restored to full working order.

*Houghton Mill near St Ives.*

*Fen skating takes place near Earith when the ice is firm enough.*

# 9
# Events

**Cambridge Festival.** Telephone: 0223 357851.
This festival, mainly of music, is held for two weeks in July. The international programme includes orchestral concerts, folk music, chamber music, jazz, soloists, organ and instrumental recitals and makes use of college halls and chapels as well as a variety of locations in the city, including the newly converted Corn Exchange concert hall. There are also special drama productions, art exhibitions and films, and elaborate feasts are held in some of the colleges.

**Cambridge Midsummer Fair**
Held on Midsummer Common by the riverside, this is the only survivor of the famous old fairs of Cambridge. For many centuries it took second place to the enormous fair at Stourbridge, a mile downstream, which from the sixteenth to the eighteenth century was probably the greatest fair in England. Stourbridge Fair ended in 1855 but Midsummer Fair is still a popular and lively event.

**Cambridge rowing and punting**
The three main rowing events take place during the year on the Cam within 3 miles (5 km) of the centre of Cambridge. In February the University Lent Races are held, followed in June by the more prestigious May Races (Cambridge holds its May Balls in June as

well, marking the end of the Summer Term). The Town Races take place in July. The course is the same for all; from Post Reach above Baits Bite Lock to the end of Long Reach on the approach to the city. The Cam is too narrow to permit racing abreast so all the events are bumping races. The total entry, perhaps about 150 boats, is sorted into divisions with about fifteen boats in each. They start 1½ lengths behind each other, the object being to bump the boat in front and change places with it for the next race. Races are normally run on four consecutive days. The garden of the Plough Inn at Fen Ditton is a favourite place for spectators. The university boat may be seen on the Cam but does most of its serious training on the Ouse at Ely before moving to the Thames.

Punting is a very popular activity with students, townsfolk and visitors from Easter to the autumn. Punts may be hired by the hour from boatyards close to the Magdalene Street and Silver Street bridges and you can cruise gently along the famous Backs or head upstream towards Grantchester. 'Chauffeur-driven' punts are also available from the Silver Street bridge.

**East of England Show,** Alwalton, Peterborough PE2 0XE. Telephone: 0733 234451.
The East of England Agricultural Society's

41

Summer Show, a three-day event, takes place every July on the showground at Alwalton, 5 miles (8 km) west of Peterborough. As well as agricultural events there are displays, trade shows, entertainments and a host of other activities. The showground covers 300 acres (120 ha) and there is parking for thirty thousand vehicles. Other items on the annual programme include shire horse, pony and hunter shows, motor sports and speedway, a steam fair, antiques fairs and trade fairs.

**Ely Festival**

The festival takes place annually in September with a varied programme of drama, music and exhibitions.

**Fen skating**

In hard winters when the ice is sufficiently firm skating championship races are held on the fens near Earith. As there can be no set dates for these, would-be spectators should keep an eye on the local press when conditions seem propitious.

**Haddenham Steam Fair**

A large steam fair is held annually in the village during the month of September.

**Reach Fair**

The remote little village of Reach has been the site of an annual fair since before 1201 when King John re-granted the right to hold a fair on Rogationtide. For centuries Reach was a small inland port which gave it a trading importance it has since lost. The Mayor of Cambridge still opens Reach Fair on May Day bank holiday, although the event is now on a small scale.

*A punt approaches the Bridge of Sighs on the Cambridge Backs.*

# 10
# Cambridge

Cambridge was not especially important in early history. There is evidence of scattered settlements before the Romans came, including burial urns, bronze tools and traces of farms and fortifications, but nothing spectacular. Under the Romans a small township developed around the site of the present Shire Hall with a road junction and a ford across the navigable river Cam or Granta. Defences were built, but the town was not strongly fortified. After the Romans left the town seems to have declined. In AD 875 there is reference to the bridge and some fifty years later Edward, son of Alfred, having reconquered the area from the Danes, moved the town to south of the river, where it grew rapidly between the Cam and the King's Ditch and was served by waterborne trade. Cambridge then gained importance as the county town, and a law court, market and mint soon followed. Despite a setback when it was burnt by the Vikings the town continued to grow; Doomsday Book records ten churches and four mills and adds that William the Conqueror destroyed 27 houses to build a castle on the site of the Roman town. The castle mound faces Shire Hall today. By the end of the eleventh century Cambridge was a major trading centre with several wharves and guilds of craftsmen. Sturbridge Fair, later to become the greatest fair in England, began about this time.

Several religious houses were founded in Cambridge in Norman times, notably Barnwell Priory, of which a chapel still survives, St Radegund's, later absorbed into Jesus College, and the Hospital of St John. Dominicans, Franciscans and Carmelites also moved into the town, and early in the thirteenth century students arrived, mostly to study for the church. They lived in hostels and their lives required discipline and organisation. The elements of a university came into being.

The subsequent history of the town is largely dominated by the history of the university. Relationships between town and gown have been often uneasy and sometimes hostile. For the undergraduates the town provided distractions from study; at one time any woman seen with an undergraduate could be arrested by the proctors as a prostitute. Until the nineteenth century Cambridge remained a huddled, busy market town of narrow streets, earning most of its income from supplying the demands of the wealthy colleges. Otherwise much of the town's importance came from its geographical position as it was a convenient halt on north-south or east-west journeys. This led to the establishment of a large number of inns, including the Falcon, the Angel, the Rose, the Red Lion, the Black Bear, the Eagle, the Blue Boar, all with many rooms, galleries and yards. Rose Crescent and the Red Lion shopping precinct are built on the yards of their respective inns.

The Civil War brought Cambridge into national prominence. Oliver Cromwell, a graduate of Sidney Sussex, was a member of Parliament for the town and in 1642 it became the headquarters of the Eastern Association at the centre of the Parliamentary cause. Eleven college heads were dismissed, three of them being imprisoned. Bridges were demolished, funds sequestrated, prisoners were housed in St John's and the dreadful William Dowsing was let loose to destroy statues, altars, crosses and pictures in the college chapels. Most of the colleges remained loyal to the King, apart from Emmanuel and Sidney Sussex which had strong Puritan sympathies, and the Restoration was generally welcomed with enthusiasm, especially by those restored to their posts.

Physical improvements to the town began following an Act of 1788 to improve paving, cleansing and lighting. However, corruption was widespread amongst the aldermen and freemen, following the example set by John Mortlock III, Mayor of Cambridge thirteen times, the first Cambridge banker and a notorious manipulator, and by his sons, two of whom held the mayoralty for fourteen years between them. Members of the Corporation milked the town of revenue and property, spending three times more on dinners than they did on public works. In 1834 elections for aldermen and councillors were introduced and a regular police force was set up. Soon Cambridge began to recover from years of depredation. The railway arrived in 1845, the station, as at Oxford, being placed at the edge of the town by the requirement of the university. The town then expanded rapidly with several streets of poor quality housing being built in Barnwell and Romsey Town, soon to become slums, unhygienic and overcrowded. In the centre a free library was opened, Silver Street Bridge was replaced and in 1874 the Corn Exchange was built, an elaborate coloured brick edifice with a glass and iron roof, now converted into a concert hall.

Recent decades have seen continued growth and prosperity with the influx of new industries, the establishment of an airport and the creation of large housing estates in the suburbs. Many new 'high tech' industries have developed here, often in co-operation with the university. Agricultural research is also a main preoccupation. Much of the Victorian industrial housing has been smartened up and taken

*The Senate House, Cambridge University.*

over by young executives, many of whom move on to restored cottages in the villages nearby. Two shopping precincts have been built: the Red Lion in the city centre, incorporating the County Library, and the Grafton Centre a mile away. Fortunately the many open spaces in and near the centre — Parker's Piece, Midsummer Common, Jesus Green, Sheeps' Green and Lammas Land — have all survived, and the 'Backs' and college grounds also provide refuge from the traffic and tumult.

There is a thriving market every weekday in the city centre, especially good for fruit and vegetables. Trinity Street, King's Parade, Sidney Street and St Andrew's Street have some excellent shops and Cambridge is particularly rich in bookshops. On any exploration of the city try not to miss Portugal Place, north of the centre, and Orchard Street on the east side, two charming examples of domestic building at its best.

Some regular Cambridge events are mentioned in chapter 9 and a good introduction to the town is provided by 'Cambridge View — a Film Guide' at the Meeting Room, St Botolph's Church, Trumpington Street, telephone: 0223 64777.

### The University of Cambridge

There is no one building that can be defined as 'Cambridge University'. Instead there is a collection of 31 colleges, several administrative buildings, faculty buildings and libraries, laboratories, the vast University Library, museums, offices, departments, playing fields,

boathouses, observatories, farms — a massive, loosely knit organisation that developed from 'schools' of scholars set up by various religious houses in the twelfth and thirteenth centuries. By 1231 Cambridge was being referred to as a university with scholars living in hostels or inns, and in 1284 the first college, Peterhouse, was founded by Hugh de Balsham, Bishop of Ely, on the lines of Merton College, the earliest foundation in Oxford.

Following Peterhouse there were four main phases of college foundation in Cambridge, starting in the fourteenth century with Michaelhouse (1324, later absorbed into Trinity College); Clare (1326); King's Hall (1337, later absorbed into Trinity College); Pembroke (1347); Gonville Hall (1348, later amalgamated with Caius); Trinity Hall (1350); and Corpus Christi (1352). Nearly one hundred years later came King's College (1441), followed by Queens (1448); St Catherine's (1473); Jesus (1496); Christ's (1505); St John's (1509); Magdalene (1542); Trinity (1546); Caius (1557); Emmanuel (1584) and Sidney Sussex (1595).

There was then a gap of over two hundred years before the foundation of Downing (1809) and three further colleges: Newnham (1871) and Girton (1873) — both originally for ladies only, now mixed, and Selwyn (1882). Colleges founded in the twentieth century are: New Hall (1954); Churchill (1960); Fitzwilliam (1966); Homerton (1977, originally a college of education); and Robinson (1977).

There are also colleges for graduates only (Darwin, Clare Hall, Hughes Hall, Wolfson,

St Edmund's House and Lucy Cavendish), and four theological colleges: Ridley Hall, Westcott House, Westminster and Wesley House. In total there are just under twelve thousand full-time students at Cambridge, of whom almost ten thousand are undergraduates. 51 per cent are studying science or science-related subjects.

A college is a self-governing body with its own Master, its Fellows (which it elects) and its undergraduates (which it selects by examination or A level results and interviews). The college is largely responsible for the teaching of its students, through supervisors and tutors, but lectures, science practicals and examinations are organised through the subject faculties which are responsible to the university. Many of the colleges are also large landowners with estates and property in and around Cambridge and elsewhere. Wealthy colleges, such as St John's and Trinity, contribute to the central funding of the university while poorer colleges draw from it. The university itself, with a total income of about £90 million, greatly depends upon government grants. The colleges pay their Fellows a stipend while the university pays the salaries of professors, lecturers (who are usually also Fellows) and the large non-academic staff.

On ceremonial occasions the university takes precedence and becomes visible in the persons of its principal officers headed by the Vice-Chancellor (an elected head of a college and the chief spokesman of the university) or perhaps even by the Chancellor, the titular head, at this time the Duke of Edinburgh. Otherwise the university officers are at work behind the scenes and the colleges take the public eye, with their splendid and impressive buildings and gardens, their activities on playing field and river, their May Balls, dramatic presentations, concerts and other events. Only at Twickenham, Lord's, Wembley and most of all between Putney and Mortlake on the Thames does the university manifest itself before the general public, arousing passions in the hearts of thousands who never attended it or its perennial rival, Oxford.

The colleges do not specialise in particular subjects although some of them from time to time acquire reputations of excellence in different areas of study. Overall, statistics may show that students of one college may do better in final examinations than students of another, but academic results league tables are no more consistent than the lower divisions of the Football League. Each college has its own character, created by the philosophy and admissions policy of its governing body, the influence of its architecture, the standard of its kitchens and the personality of its head porter, but this may not be discernible to the outsider. The obvious differences between colleges are in their size and the splendour of the buildings. Fortunately in Cambridge access to the colleges is subject to few restrictions and the visitor is free to enjoy what may be seen.

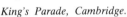

*King's Parade, Cambridge.*

## The Cambridge Science Park

The Cambridge Science Park was established in 1970 by Trinity College on a site owned by the college on the northern edge of the city. There are now fifty firms operating on the 130 acre (52.5 ha) site with staffs ranging from three to 299. The Science Park is a notable example of university and industry co-operation; many of the firms are on the frontiers of scientific and technological progress and are able to make use of the university's experience and expertise. The Trinity Centre provides a bar, common room and meeting rooms for those working on the Park.

A Business Park is being developed on land to the east of the Science Park.

## A walk around Cambridge

This walk begins and ends at the multi-storey car park off Jesus Lane. It is usually possible to leave a car here with little or no delay except during the summer season between 11 am and 3 pm, when some waiting may be necessary. The route takes you into many of the colleges but at certain times during the year, for example during the summer examination period or when preparations for May Balls are in hand, some colleges may be closed to visitors or access may be limited. The colleges are private property but in general visitors are welcome provided that they observe the requirements. Because of the influx of coach parties of tourists, summer is not the best time for visiting Cambridge. Indeed the famous Backs, so crowded in July and August, are at their best in springtime and autumn.

Leave the car park by the Bridge Street exit and turn right, noting the finely restored upper storeys of the buildings on this side of the road. Cross Magdalene Bridge over the Cam and arrive at the sixteenth-century brick frontage of **Magdalene College,** the last of Cambridge's colleges to permit the admission of women students. Magdalene has a beautiful garden, an attractive hall and in the second court the famous Pepys Library, housing the diary of Samuel Pepys and the three thousand volumes he bequeathed to the college.

From Magdalene continue past a row of interesting shops — a good example of a seventeenth-century town street that has been spared the excesses of modernisation. Across the traffic lights are the **Folk Museum and Kettle's Yard** (see chapter 7). Turn left into Northampton Street and in about 300 yards (275 metres) enter the grounds of **St John's College** through the ornamental iron gates. St John's, one of the larger colleges, has much to offer. To the left is the School of Pythagoras, or Merton Hall, one of the oldest buildings in the city dating from about 1200. Close by and in great contrast is the Cripps Building, a notable example of modern university architecture. Dominating the gardens is New Court, completed in 1831, the largest college building up to that time. The elaborate lantern with its delicate pinnacles is familiarly known as the Wedding Cake. New Court is connected with the older buildings over the river by the famous Bridge of Sighs (1831) although the visitor uses the Old Bridge of 1712. Across the river are three connecting courts built between 1511 and 1671, the library and hall. First Court and the splendid gatehouse were the earliest of the college buildings. The large chapel is an ambitious Victorian creation by Sir George Gilbert Scott and makes no attempt to accord

*Clare College, Cambridge.*

46

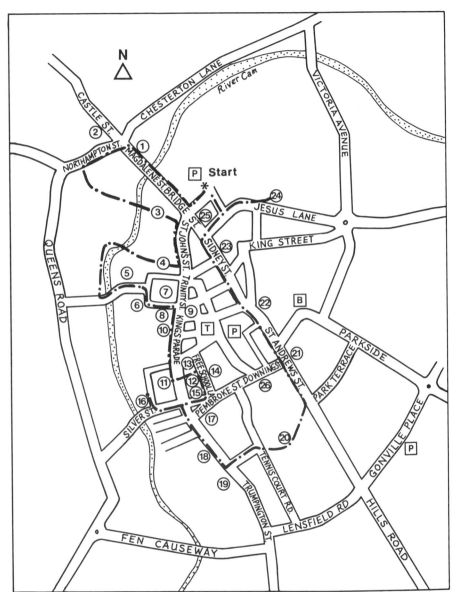

*Plan of central Cambridge, showing the course of the walk suggested in the text. Key: 1 Magdalene College; 2 Cambridge and County Folk Museum and Kettle's Yard; 3 St John's College; 4 Trinity College; 5 Trinity Hall; 6 Clare College; 7 Gonville and Caius College; 8 Senate House; 9 Great St Mary's church; 10 King's College; 11 St Catherine's College; 12 Corpus Christi College; 13 St Benet's church; 14 Old Cavendish Laboratory; 15 St Botolph's church; 16 Queens' College; 17 Pembroke College; 18 Peterhouse; 19 Fitzwilliam Museum; 20 Downing College; 21 Emmanuel College; 22 Christ's College; 23 Sidney Sussex College; 24 Jesus College; 25 Round Church; 26 Museum of Archaeology and Ethnology; B bus station; P car park; T tourist information centre.*

with the other college buildings.

Next to St John's is **Trinity College,** the largest college in either Cambridge or Oxford, famous not only for its buildings but for the extraordinary number of poets, scientists and scholars it has fostered. Henry VIII's foundation of Trinity incorporated two older colleges, King's Hall and Michaelhouse. Buildings of King's Hall, founded by Edward III, stand on either side of the Great Gate, which rivals St John's gatehouse as the most splendid entry in Cambridge. Trinity Great Court impresses by its sheer spaciousness; it includes the Combination Rooms, hall, Master's Lodge, Old Library, King Edward's Tower and the chapel and in the centre is a spectacular fountain. In the antechapel statues of varying quality commemorate some of the most famous Trinity men: Sir Isaac Newton, by Roubiliac, 1755, stands surveying Bacon, Barrow, Macaulay, Whewell and Tennyson. Byron, Thackeray, J. J. Thomson and Rutherford are a few more famous names from Trinity's past.

Much of Trinity was built under the mastership of Thomas Nevile (1593-1615). He laid out the design of Great Court and added Nevile's Court to the west. The library was added to this court under the mastership of Isaac Barrow and was designed by Sir Christopher Wren. His classically styled building houses one of the world's great libraries and it is worth organising a visit to coincide with the period when it is open to visitors (check times with the porters' lodge).

Cross the Cam by Trinity Bridge, walk through the avenue of limes and return across the river by Garret Hostel Bridge for entrancing views of the college Backs and the other Cam bridges. Garret Hostel Lane leads to **Trinity Hall** on the right, a smaller college whose old buildings are semi-concealed beneath eighteenth- and nineteenth-century refacing and restoration. The chapel and library are worth visiting. Next to Trinity Hall is **Clare College** with its fine seventeenth-century court and eighteenth-century chapel. Clare Bridge is the oldest of the Cam bridges and leads to the beautifully maintained gardens. Much of Clare's accommodation is on the far side of Queens' Road opposite the University Library.

Return through Clare, turning left along the lane and then right to the centre of the university's administration, the Old Schools. Opposite is **Gonville and Caius College** (pronounced 'keys'). Dr John Caius, royal physician of the mid sixteenth century, refounded Gonville Hall in 1557 and became Master. He added Caius Court and built three gates, of Humility, Virtue and Honour, marking out the path for his students to follow. They entered the college through the Gate of Humility, a

*The Gate of Honour, Gonville and Caius College, Cambridge.*

simple structure now removed to the Master's garden and replaced in Victorian times, walked the path to the Gate of Virtue, an ambitious Italianate construction with on the far side a reference to Wisdom, and left the college by the Gate of Honour to take their degree. This gate is a remarkably complex design executed apparently in miniature and is one of Cambridge's happiest extravagances.

Beyond the Gate of Honour are the Senate House and the Old Schools — the university as opposed to the colleges. The classical **Senate House,** designed by James Gibbs and built in 1722-30, is an appropriate setting for the degree ceremonies when the university dignitaries appear in full academic splendour. Across from the Senate House is the university church, **Great St Mary's** (see chapter 5), with the Market Square behind it. To the right is one of the world's most famous streets, **King's Parade,** mercifully no longer a through route for traffic, with a varied collection of shops and cafés. St Edward's

Passage leads off the Parade to a quiet and pleasant square with St Edward's church (chapter 5) in its centre.

The west side of King's Parade is dominated by a superb chestnut tree and by Cambridge's most spectacular building, **King's College** chapel. Enter King's through William Wilkins's carefully detailed and theatrically effective gatehouse and screen of the 1820s and see how neatly the differing styles of architecture in King's Great Court blend, not competing with the grandeur of the chapel but complementing it. The chapel itself was built in three phases between 1446 and 1515 and maintains a remarkable unity inside and out. Nearly 300 feet (91 metres) long and rising to a height of 80 feet (24 metres) inside, the sheer scale of the building makes the first unforgettable impression. Exploration of the interior reveals the consummate detail of the stonework with royal crowns, portcullises and Tudor roses everywhere, and above all the intricate symmetry of the fan vaulting. The windows installed between 1515 and 1531 picture the life of the Virgin Mary and the story of Christ, together with the Old Testament prophecies foretelling these events. Other outstanding features are the magnificent screen and the Rubens painting 'Adoration of the Magi' given to the college in 1962 and now placed behind the altar. An exhibition showing how and why the chapel was built occupies the northern side chapels and descriptive guides are available from the sales counter. The famous choir sings evensong on most days of the week.

Like Wilkins, James Gibbs did not try to rival the chapel when he came to design the Fellows Building but simply used the typical classical style of his time and his straightforward three-storey range, like that of Clare College on the other side, enhances the architecture of the chapel without distracting from it.

King's next-door neighbour is St **Catherine's College,** with pleasant but not distinguished buildings. Opposite is **Corpus Christi,** founded by two town guilds originally for citizens of Cambridge. The first court, New Court, was designed by Wilkins in formal style. Past the hall is Old Court, the oldest surviving quadrangle in Cambridge, built when the college was founded in 1352 but unfortunately altered rather clumsily in succeeding centuries. A passage from Old Court, where the dramatists Marlowe and Fletcher had rooms, leads to St **Benet's church** (chapter 5), which served as the college chapel for its first two hundred years. From the churchyard turn into Free School Lane, which runs along the back of Corpus Christi. On the left is the world-famous **Old Cavendish Laboratory** where the Physics Department was based until it moved to new premises on the western edge of Cambridge. Here some of the most momentous discoveries of modern times were made by physicists including Clerk Maxwell, Thomson and Lord Rutherford. The building now houses the Department of Aerial Photography.

St Botolph's Lane leads back to the main road, now called Trumpington Street, with **St**

*Old Court, Corpus Christi College, Cambridge.*

49

*St Benet's churchyard and Corpus Christi College, Cambridge.*

**Botolph's church** (chapter 5) opening directly on to the pavement. Cross diagonally to Silver Street; about 200 yards (180 metres) along turn right into Queens' Lane for **Queens' College,** founded by two queens, Margaret, wife of Henry VII and Elizabeth Woodville, wife of Edward IV. The fine gatehouse leads into the mid-fifteenth century First Court, comparatively little altered since, with the Old Hall, its interior well worth viewing. To the right is Walnut Court. Here is a richly decorated chapel of 1891 containing a fine late fifteenth-century reredos. Through First Court is Cloister Court, late fifteenth-century, with a tower on the south side where Erasmus is said to have lived in 1510. On the north side is the timbered President's Lodge, a welcome surprise in so many courts of stone and brick. A replica of James Essex's Mathematical Bridge, made solely of pegged timbers, crosses the river. The architectural merit of Queens' buildings on this side is hard to discern, although in this they are no different from many of Cambridge's more recent additions, including the University Centre that overlooks the river on the far side of Silver Street Bridge.

Return along Silver Street to Trumpington Street. On the right is the University Press and diagonally opposite is **Pembroke College.** This has suffered from its handling by the Victorian architect Waterhouse but retains a fine gateway, a chapel designed by Christopher Wren (one of his earliest works), the Old Library and some attractive gardens.

Opposite Pembroke is Little St Mary's church and the university's oldest college, **Peterhouse.** Founded in 1284, it retains few very old buildings. Although the hall dates from about 1286 it was mostly rebuilt in the Victorian era and has much interior decoration by William Morris. The chapel with its striking gables was completed in 1665 but the interior before then was largely devastated by Dowsing, the Puritan church wrecker. The Front Court is seventeenth-century.

Further down Trumpington Street is the **Fitzwilliam Museum** (see chapter 7) but this merits a visit entirely to itself. To continue with the college tour turn into Fitzwilliam Street and in Tennis Court Road enter the grounds of **Downing College.** This dates from 1807 when William Wilkins devised the impressive ranges of classical buildings in a lavishly spacious setting. The funds of the founder, Sir George Downing, were exhausted before the design was completed but appropriate additions were made in the 1870s by E. M. Barry. The twentieth-century chapel is less successful but the recent Howard Building at the west end of the college effectively reproduces the original style.

Leave Downing by the main entrance in St Andrew's Street and turn left for **Emmanuel College,** founded in 1584 for the training of Puritan preachers. A large number of its early graduates emigrated to New England, including John Harvard, founder of Harvard University. The chapel is a triumph of Christopher

50

Wren, beautifully proportioned, with superb stonework and a fresh and elegant interior. The eighteenth-century Front Court is by James Essex. Emmanuel also has extensive gardens with an ancient swimming pool, and its buildings have a harmony which later additions have enhanced rather than destroyed.

Continue northwards through the semi-pedestrianised shopping centre — a typical Cambridge compromise — to the elaborately decorated gatehouse of **Christ's College,** where Milton studied for seven years with rooms in Front Court. The Second Court has an architecturally important Fellows Building with the Fellows Garden beyond equipped with eighteenth-century bathing pool, a summerhouse, beehives, busts, memorial urns and superb trees. Christ's also owns one of the ugliest modern blocks, out of scale with the rest of the college buildings and with King Street on the other side.

Northwards past the chain stores is **Sidney Sussex College,** once attended by Oliver Cromwell. Much of the College was rebuilt in the nineteenth century and the garden is possibly its most attractive feature. Sidney is only a few yards from the Round Church and the car park, but if time permits turn into Jesus Lane for the short walk to **Jesus College.** This stands like a fortress in its own spacious grounds and fine gardens. It was built by Bishop Alcock of Ely on the site of St Radegund's Convent and incorporates some of the convent buildings including the cloisters. The chapel is a remodelling of the chancel of the original priory church and some of the greatest Victorian architects and decorators, including William Morris, Pugin and Bodley, were involved in the work, creating one of Cambridge's most elaborate and colourful interiors with craftsmanship of the highest order.

Return along Jesus Lane and turn right for the car park.

This walk will take between four and five hours, longer if the weather is fine and time is taken strolling along the Backs or perhaps exploring some of the interiors, chapels, halls and libraries open to view. There is much more to see in Cambridge, including the newer colleges and the museums (chapter 7). Good examples of the more recent foundations are Fitzwilliam College in Huntingdon Road, Churchill College in Storey's Way and Robinson College in Grange Road; it should be easy to park near each of these. At certain times it is possible to tour the great University Library in West Road. The History Faculty Library in Sidgwick Avenue should be seen by anyone interested in controversial modern architecture.

*Gardens, St John's College*

51

# 11
# Cities, towns and villages

With over one hundred villages in South Cambridgeshire District alone, it is possible here to give only a sample of Cambridgeshire villages. No place in the county is devoid of interest and all are worth exploring.

## BARNACK

This large village 4 miles (6.5 km) south-east of Stamford is the site of a famous medieval quarry known as the Field of Hills and Holes. Barnack Rag quarried here was transported overland to the river Nene near Castor and thence by river and medieval canal to Ely, Cambridge, Bury St Edmunds and further afield. The quarry was worked out by the end of the fifteenth century and is now a national nature reserve. Some of the handsome older buildings in the village as well as the parish church of St John Baptist (chapter 5) are made of the local stone. There is a tower mill one mile (1.6 km) to the west of the village (see chapter 8).

## BARRINGTON

The village developed around an enormous green, once even larger than it is now as seventeenth-century building has encroached upon it. There are several thatched cottages and a fine large church, All Saints, with much thirteenth- and fourteenth-century work. Clunch, extensively used in local building, used to be quarried nearby. On the outskirts there is a vast cement works.

## BARTLOW

Bartlow is a small village by the Essex border. St Mary's church has a round Norman tower and three fine fifteenth-century wall paintings, including a splendid dragon. A path in the churchyard leads across a derelict railway (and the county boundary) to the Bartlow Hills. There were originally nine of these conical Romano-British burial mounds dating from the second century, three of which survive.

## BENWICK

This fenland village grew up on the raised banks of an extinct river which once flowed along the line of the High Street, turning right at the site of the church. It is the only settlement of any size on the black peat.

## BOURN

Readers of Doomsday Book will be familiar with Picot, the Sheriff of Cambridgeshire, despoiler of much of Cambridge and owner of land in 42 parishes, who built himself a castle in Bourn. About 1600 a fine manor house, Bourn Hall, was built within the castle earthworks. Today the hall is the home of an internationally known private fertility clinic. The church of St Helen and St Mary has work from the twelfth century onwards. The strong tower is topped by an odd twisted little spire. Inside is a medieval rood-screen and stalls and benches from the sixteenth century, as well as a maze. Bourn Mill, the oldest in the county, is on the Caxton Road (see chapter 8).

## BRAMPTON

Adjacent to Huntingdon, the old village has been largely overwhelmed by modern building and the establishment of an RAF station in the park. Samuel Pepys spent much of his childhood in 44 Huntingdon Road, now known as Pepys House, and in later years used to visit the Black Bull. In the old forge in the High Street is a small museum. A path from St Mary's church leads to the large open meadow of Portholme.

## BUCKDEN

Until 1961 the Great North Road ran through Buckden, which explains the presence of two large hotels, once coaching inns, the Lion and the George, almost opposite each other. The Lion, once the Lion and Lamb, is the older, parts of it dating from about 1500. Behind a long red-brick wall is Buckden Palace, once owned by the Bishops of Lincoln. The Great Tower and the inner and outer gatehouses date from the late fifteenth century; the rest of the buildings are comparatively recent apart from the Great Hall. Buckden was popular with the bishops, but after the Lincoln diocese was divided in 1837 the palace was sold to a private owner. In 1957 the Roman Catholic Church bought it and it now houses Claretian missionaries. St Mary's church (see chapter 5) stands a few yards from the tower.

## BURWELL

This is a large fen-edge village, about 2 miles (3 km) long, with a remarkable church (see chapter 5), the site of a castle where Earl Geoffrey de Mandeville was killed in 1144 when leading a rebellion against King Stephen, many interesting old houses and the remains of an inland port. The castle, to the west of the church, was never completed; its buildings were used for a time by the Abbots of Ramsey but have all vanished leaving a pleasant grassy sward. Notable examples of the older houses are 4 and 6 High Street, now one dwelling, standing by a small green at the Cambridge end of the village, and Parsonage

Farm on Low Road with some fascinating outbuildings. Watch out for Open Day when many of the houses are open to visitors. Hythe Lane leads to the old public wharf on Burwell Lode, a seventeenth-century waterway still navigable by small craft. There were over twenty basins and short canals serving the waterborne trade until well into the twentieth century. The bank of the lode makes a bracing walk past the sites of a fertiliser factory and the brickworks, both served by barges and lighters for many decades. The pale Burwell brick is much in evidence in buildings hereabouts.

## CAMBRIDGE
See chapter 10.

## CAXTON
The A14 (Ermine Street) now carries comparatively little traffic compared with other main roads in the vicinity and all that most motorists see of Caxton is the replica gibbet by the A45 roundabout outside a pub. The village itself is a mile to the south and was once a major posting station on the old London road. Caxton Manor used to be the George Inn; its Georgian frontage conceals much Elizabethan work. Crown House was once the Crown Inn and is of similar date. St Andrew's church, south-west of the village, dates back to the late thirteenth century and the original village was grouped around it.

## CHATTERIS
This is a small fenland town built mostly of the local yellow brick. There was a religious

foundation here in Saxon times but little connection with the outside world, except by water, until 1643 when the road to Ely, now the A142, was built to Cromwell's orders by Henry Ireton. It is still known as Ireton's Way. Chatteris seems to breed fighting men; two famous British boxers, Eric Boon and Dave 'Boy' Green, came from here and George William Clare VC is commemorated in the church.

## CHIPPENHAM
Much of the medieval village was destroyed when Lord Orford created his park in the late seventeenth century. He replaced the lost cottages by a row of new ones on the road to Badingham, making Chippenham one of the very earliest estate villages. Opposite the church is a handsome school in Dutch style built in 1714, and some early nineteenth-century semi-detached cottages. St Margaret's church is full of interest and atmosphere and contains a splendid wall painting of St Christopher. Lord Orford's mansion in the park was demolished by a later owner and the present house dates from 1886. A mile (1.6 km) west of the village is Chippenham Fen, one of the best preserved areas of peat fen.

## COMBERTON
This large village has much modern building, including a good village college, but retains some attractive cottages. St Mary's church is notable for some exceptional medieval bench-ends. The Old Vicarage nearby incorporates a medieval hall.

*The derelict manor house at Croxton.*

## COTTENHAM

The long main street of Cottenham lies on the old route between Cambridge and the fens. At the north end is All Saints' church, its strong tower topped by onion-shaped pinnacles reminiscent of the Kremlin, with embattlements everywhere. This site was probably chosen because it was firm ground above flood level and convenient for unloading building stone brought by barge along Cottenham Lode. The green is over a mile away at the south end. Major fires in 1676 and 1850 destroyed much of Cottenham and explain the similarities in style of many of the houses. The village was once famous for its cheese, recorded as early as in 1280, but its manufacture ceased after outbreaks of cattle plague in 1865-6. Point-to-point meetings are held nearby in the winter months. A detailed history of Cottenham and its neighbours Landbeach and Waterbeach, *Liable to Floods,* has been written by J. R. Ravensdale.

## CROXTON

On the south side of the St Neots road about 13 miles (21 km) from Cambridge is the handful of cottages, mostly seventeenth- and eighteenth-century, that is now Croxton. Some of the cottages are empty and decaying, half hidden behind unkempt gardens. The manor house, a late medieval hall with later remodelling, is crumbling away by a small overgrown green. A lane leads to Croxton Park, a solid eighteenth-century rebuilding of an Elizabethan mansion. St James's church is set among fine trees 150 yards (137 metres) south of the Park, much of it thirteenth century with a later tower. The church overlooks the site of an earlier village of Croxton, many traces of which still existed in the early nineteenth century.

## DOWNHAM

This is Downham in the Isle, or Little Downham, not to be confused with Downham Market across the border in Norfolk. It lies on the edge of the Isle of Ely. St Leonard's church has Norman work in the tower and a fascinating Norman south doorway with 26 carved heads. Tower Farm, on the north-west of the village, incorporates the remains of the Bishop's Palace, a favourite residence of Bishops of Ely in early times although unused by them since 1642. The surviving buildings were erected by Bishop Alcock (1486-1500). The adjacent barn has been converted into a restaurant. About 2½ miles (4 km) along the Wisbech Road (B1411) is the embankment of the New Bedford, or Hundred Foot, River; the Hundred Foot pumping station with its historically interesting inscriptions is a few hundred yards further on.

## DUXFORD

Wedged between the river Cam and the M11, Duxford is a large village with several attractively restored thatched cottages, many of them housing executives from the nearby industrial undertakings. There are two churches: St Peter's is the parish church, standing on the edge of the village, its Norman tower overlooking the water meadows. By the village green is St John's, a redundant church, also with a Norman tower and an interior well worth exploring, if you can locate the key. The John Barleycorn inn has a fine frontage dated 1660. The gardens of the beautifully restored Duxford Mill are open on occasions in the summer.

To the north of the village across the A505 and close to Whittlesford station are Duxford Chapel (see chapter 6) and the Red Lion Inn. The Red Lion has finely carved early Tudor beams in some of the downstairs rooms and is an attractively rambling building. It reputedly sheltered James I when he was taken ill returning from Newmarket in 1619.

For Duxford Airfield, now part of the Imperial War Museum, see chapter 7.

## EARITH

On the east side of the village is a vital element of fen drainage, as here the Old and New Bedford rivers, cut by Vermuyden in the mid seventeenth century, leave the main river Ouse and run in almost parallel lines 21 miles (33.75 km) north-east to rejoin the Ouse at Denver. The bypassed section of river which circles eastward through Ely and Littleport is called the Old West and entrance to it is controlled by Hermitage Lock. The long, narrow stretch of land between the Bedford rivers is the Ouse Washes (see chapter 2). Traces of a Civil War earthwork known as the Bulwark can be made out from the causeway at Earith.

## ELSWORTH

Now a village of comfortable size and appearance, Elsworth was originally a forest clearing belonging to one Eli. The village developed along a watercourse which still flows through Brook Street, although much diminished since the fens were drained. A Jurassic limestone outcrop brought university geologists to Elsworth until the site was built over in recent years. The rough grassed area by the manor house is known as the Ware and is the site of the medieval moated manor. There are several attractive old houses and cottages, notably Dear's Farm in Fardell's Lane, Low Farm (built in 1595 and at one time a workhouse) in Brook Street, and Ivyfold in Broad End. Holy Trinity church stands on a small rise. Much of the fabric is fourteenth-century and there are some early Tudor stalls

*Medieval monastic buildings at Ely.*

in excellent condition. An informative guide to church and village is obtainable in the church.

### ELTON

There are several fine seventeenth-century houses here and Elton Hall (chapter 6) is half a mile (800 metres) to the south. On the west side of the village is the river Nene with a lock attractively situated by the old mill buildings.

### ELY

*Early closing Tuesday; market day Thursday.*

Dominated but not quite overwhelmed by its massive cathedral (chapter 5), Ely is an intriguing little city and market town with much to offer. It extends up a hillside — the steep shore of the Isle. At the foot is the Great Ouse, the trim quayside usually busy with boats, the Cutter Inn and the handsome maltings now converted into a multi-purpose hall. At the top of the hill are the cathedral, the green with its cannon, the parish church of St Mary, an exceptional range of medieval buildings, some housing cathedral clergy and others incorporated into the King's School, and a few fine Georgian houses. In between are a good collection of shops, restaurants, pubs and cafés, a despoiled market square, some finely restored old cottages and ample free car parking.

A tour of Ely might begin at St Mary's, next to timbered Cromwell House, where Oliver Cromwell lived for some years, and opposite the Old Fire Engine House, now a restaurant and art gallery. Cross Palace Green with the old Bishop's Palace, now a Sue Ryder home, on the right, turn along the street called The Gallery to the right of the cathedral and enter the Porta, once the gate of the Benedictine priory on this site, dating from the end of the fourteenth century. This leads into the park; to the right is the fifteenth-century Monks' Granary and beyond is the site of a motte and bailey castle built by the rebel barons against Stephen in the civil war. To the left are several medieval buildings, now part of King's School, including the Prior's House, the Queen's Hall, Prior Crauden's Chapel — a beautiful, richly decorated little chapel accessible by a spiral staircase — and, further along, the remains of the Infirmary and the Cellarer's House. To the right are Walsingham House, built for Adam of Walsingham, designer of the octagon, Powcher's Hall and the Black Hostelry, originally a hostel for visiting Benedictine monks. Return to the Porta and walk through the park, with superb views of the cathedral, to Broad Street. On the far side is the Three Blackbirds, the oldest house in Ely. Take a lane down to the river and turn left to Waterside, which has several attractive restored cottages. Turn up Fore Hill to the market place, where the only early buildings to survive are the White Hart and Archer House. Carry on up the High

55

*Godmanchester: the Great Ouse and the 'Chinese' bridge.*

Street; on the left are more medieval buildings, the Almonry, Sacristy, Goldsmith's Tower and, now incorporating a craft shop and café, Steeple Gate. At the top of High Street turn left for the west door of the cathedral and Palace Green.

If time allows, return to St Mary's, cross St Mary Street and turn left and then right into West End to see two more ancient buildings, part of St John's Farm. They date from about 1240 and were part of the hospitals of St John and St Mary Magdalene.

## FENSTANTON

There are several good houses in the village and an interesting church, St Peter and St Paul, which contains the tomb of the famous landscape garden designer Lancelot 'Capability' Brown, who was lord of the manor here from 1768 to 1783. Its best known feature, however, is the lock-up with its portentous clock tower in the village centre. This square red-brick structure dates from the late seventeenth century.

## FOWLMERE

Fowlmere is a compact village close to the Bran Ditch, a defensive work designed to protect the Icknield Way. The name means 'mere of the wild fowl' and there is an RSPB reserve a mile west of the village. St Mary's church is mostly fourteenth-century. Fowlmere seems always to have been well endowed with inns and indeed still is, although they are now better known for their restaurants than as good pull-ups for coaches and post-chaises.

## FOXTON

The long main street has several good timber-framed cottages and is especially attractive around the tiny green. Nearby there was an iron age settlement and traces of a Roman villa have been found. The village became widely known with the publication in 1975 of a readable and stimulating history, *The Common Stream,* by a resident, Rowland Parker.

## FULBOURN

There are several interesting sites close to this village, which has plenty of thatched cottages and pleasant old houses as well as much Cambridge suburban development. Fulbourn Fen, an educational nature reserve (chapter 2), lies to the east and two areas with public access, the Beechwood and Wandlebury (chapters 2 and 4), are within 2 miles (3 km). A mill open at times to the public (chapter 8) is half a mile (800 metres) to the west. The large Victorian building on the Cambridge road is a mental hospital. St Vigor's church has some interesting brasses and much thirteenth- and fourteenth-century work.

## GAMLINGAY

No fewer than 58 buildings in the village are listed by the Royal Commission on Historical Monuments. Especially interesting are Emplins, close to the church, a timbered house of the fifteenth and sixteenth centuries, and Merton Manor Farm, of the same period with a pigeon house and seventeenth-century barn.

In Church Street is a fine row of ten alms-houses dating from 1665 with a chapel added on the end. St Mary's church is mainly thirteenth-century, a confident battlemented building with tower and chancel of the local sandstone quarried in Stocks Lane in the village. The whitewashed interior has a good Perpendicular screen and a set of stalls dating from about 1442. The remarkable table in the vestry is the sounding board of a seventeenth-century pulpit. Gamlingay was a market town of local importance until much of the centre was destroyed by fire in 1600, when the market moved to nearby Potton.

Gamlingay Cinques Nature Reserve (chapter 2) is north-west of the village by the Cinques Road/B1040 junction and south-west is Gamlingay meadow, a small remnant of the Great Heath. North of the village is a vineyard where wine may be sampled and bought.

## GODMANCHESTER

Godmanchester was the principal Roman centre in the Ouse valley with a fort, lodgings, a bath-house and later a town hall. It became an important road junction with three major roads meeting here, Ermine Street, the *Via Devana* and a military road. Some of the relics from this period can be seen locally in the museums at St Ives and Longsands School, St Neots (chapter 7). Later it became a busy market town and a royal manor with a charter granted by King John in 1212. Today God-manchester is a large village — or small town — much of it a conservation area, still busy with traffic and rich in the heritage of many centuries. Its best known feature is the 'Chinese' bridge (built in 1827 and restored in 1979) leading to a walk along the riverside to Godmanchester Lock and the great meadow of Portholme. Another and older 'Chinese' bridge is in the grounds of Island Hall (see chapter 6), one of many fine houses in Post Street, the road to Huntingdon; others include the bookshop and the Quaker Centre (both once inns), Island Cottage, the Red House and the Black Bull. Other notable buildings are Farm Hall in West Street, Porch Farm in London Road, the old Queen Elizabeth School building now used by the local council, and three fine houses in Earning Street, Plantagenet House, The Gables (1628) with a timbered barn and large dovecot, and Tudor House (1603), now sadly empty and in need of urgent repair. The houses facing the river along the Causeway make a specially attractive group.

Chadley Lane, one of Godmanchester's oldest streets, with a very old house (restored) on the left, leads to St Mary's church. This is mostly thirteenth- to fifteenth-century but the two small lancets above the screen indicate the width of the Norman nave. Interesting fea-tures include the misericords beneath the fifteenth-century choir stalls with finely executed carvings of animals and people and, outside, the Saxon mass dial in the chancel wall. The tower was rebuilt in 1623. The words 'Burgus Gumcestr' beneath the badge of corporation above the west door refer to the early alternative name of the town, *Gumecestre*.

## GRANTCHESTER

Just over 2 miles (3 km) from Cambridge — there is a popular walk alongside the river — Grantchester is an attractive village much frequented by members of the university and famous for its connection with Rupert Brooke, who lodged at the Old Vicarage in 1909-10, when an undergraduate. The house is now owned by the best-selling novelist Jeffrey Archer. There are good, if often crowded pubs, a fifteenth-century Manor Farm with a converted pigeon house nearby, and some pretty cottages. The earliest part of the church of St Andrew and St Mary is twelfth-century; the fourteenth-century chancel is especially fine and other notable features are the tower and the north porch. Tennyson and Byron both loved Grantchester and Byron is still remembered in the name of Byron's Pool, although the setting here has been sadly altered. Brooke's mill has been burnt down and there is not much 'peace and holy quiet' in the village these days.

## HADDENHAM

The highest village in the fens, Haddenham stands on a hill of 120 feet (36.5 metres) — a veritable mountain in this area. There are a few good houses — the best is Porch House, 1657 — and a pleasant high street, although the newer building is of variable quality. Aldreth, on the south side of the village, stands on the old causeway which was once the main route between Cambridge and the fens and is associated with the defence of the fenland by Hereward the Wake. There is a good Farmland Museum in the High Street (chapter 7). The much restored Holy Trinity church dates from the late thirteenth century and contains a replica of Ovin's Stone; the original, part of Ovin's memorial cross dating from about AD 673, is now in Ely Cathedral, having been discovered in use as a mounting block in Haddenham. The church lacks a spire; money for one was collected locally in the nineteenth century but was apparently embezzled by an ancestor of the writer's wife who then speedily emigrated to America.

## HASLINGFIELD

Once pilgrims came to make offerings here to Our Lady of White Hill but of the site of the chapel there is now no trace. Haslingfield Hall was built by Thomas Wendy, Henry VIII's physician, in the 1550s, but much of it was demolished in the early nineteenth century. The hall's pigeon house, built in 1640 with accommodation for 1500 birds, is now converted into a handsome private dwelling. All Saints' church has a notable west tower, built about 1400, and several monuments to the Wendy family. The lead roof to the south porch, at first glance a modern repair, is actually dated 1746.

## HELPSTON

This village on the edge of the fen, with the Welland valley to the north and patches of woodland to the south and west, is in the centre of an area of much archaeological interest with evidence of earthworks and enclosure showing that this was a place of religious importance in the neolithic and bronze ages. More recently Helpston was the birthplace of the poet John Clare; the cottage in which he was born, now extended and beautifully maintained, is near the village centre. Clare's earlier poetry is a vivid commentary on the natural life and agricultural changes in the early nineteenth century. He is buried in the churchyard and a memorial to him stands opposite the village cross (about 1300) by the main crossroads.

## HEMINGFORD ABBOTS

The village is not yet submerged by modern development and retains several good thatched cottages. It once belonged to the Ramsey Abbey estate — hence the name. St Margaret's church, mainly fourteenth-century, is close to the river Ouse and its spire is familiar to navigators. At the west end of the village Meadow Lane, lined with lavish modern houses, leads to the Black Bridge (no vehicles) and a pleasant path across meadows to Houghton Mill (see chapter 8).

## HEMINGFORD GREY

Despite much undistinguished post-war building there is still some character about the village, especially in and around the High Street. Notable are River House, Broom Lodge, Glebe Cottage (1583) and Hemingford Grey House, once the rectory, with a splendid plane tree planted in 1702. The Manor House was built around a twelfth-century hall and is said to be among the oldest inhabited houses in England. St James's church is beautifully sited beside the river; it lost its spire in a hurricane in 1741. Both the Hemingfords become crowded with visitors in the summer.

## HISTON

Although suburbanised and partly industrialised, Histon has kept its green, pond and ducks and in St Andrew's has a fine church of the twelfth and thirteenth centuries with some remarkable stonework, especially in the transepts. Jam making on a commercial scale began here in 1870 but the large Chivers factory site now houses a new 'Vision Park'. Histon is the home of Unwins, the famous seed merchants, and their trial grounds, open to visitors in the spring, have become a major tourist attraction with their superb displays.

## HOUGHTON

Houghton and Wyton form one continuous village on the north bank of the Ouse. As in the Hemingfords on the opposite side, there has been much recent development and the older buildings have been generally smartened up. Houghton has lost its green but the pump remains, as does a timbered house of 1480 and a bust of Potto Brown, once tenant of the mill. Summer visitors abound here, many coming to see the mill, now owned by the National Trust (see chapter 8). The Three Jolly Butchers in Wyton dates from 1622 and contains some old wall paintings.

## HUNTINGDON

*Early closing Wednesday.*

Huntingdon developed from a river crossing by Ermine Street. It was a prosperous town in the tenth century with both a market and a mint, and as many as sixteen churches in Norman times. Although its importance later diminished, in the Civil War, when the number of churches had reduced to four, it was used as headquarters by Cromwell, who was born here, and Charles I successively. Subsequently it became an important stage-coach centre; the George is a specially handsome former coaching inn, where now annual performances of Shakespeare's plays take place in June. Until 1974 Huntingdon was the county town of England's second smallest county and, although not spacious, it preserves some feeling of civic dignity.

There has been much residential and industrial development in recent years and the population is now about 15,000. Through traffic has been diverted from the centre by a one-way ring road (as effective a deterrent for many visitors as a fortified wall), and east-west traffic hurries by on a huge flyover.

Notable buildings include the two surviving churches, St Mary's and All Saints', a town hall of 1745, the Falcon (once Cromwell's headquarters), Cromwell House, built on the site of an Augustinian friary and of an earlier house in which Cromwell was born, and Whitwell House. The Cromwell Museum (chapter 7) was once part of the grammar school which in turn was part of the medieval Hospital of St John. The poet William Cowper lived for a time at 29 High Street, now the offices of the *Hunts Post.*

*Hemingford Grey on the Great Ouse.*

Almost all recent development is on the north side of the town. To the west is Brampton, birthplace of Samuel Pepys, and Huntingdon Racecourse. South are the meadow of Portholme, once a racecourse, a cricket ground and a flying field, and Godmanchester, linked to Huntingdon by a fourteenth-century bridge over the Ouse, with the Georgian Old Bridge Hotel at one end and Keyser Bondor's mill, now tastefully converted into dwellings, at the other.

## IMPINGTON

Impington has one of England's most important school buildings, Impington Village College, designed in 1938 by two of Europe's leading architects, Walter Gropius and Maxwell Fry. It is a pleasing and workmanlike complex that set the pattern for much subsequent school building. Today, much extended, it is a comprehensive school for about a thousand pupils. The village college concept of a secondary school serving several villages, and also providing facilities for adult education and the cultural needs of the community, was devised by Henry Morris, a director of education for the county, and there are examples of these pioneering colleges, now all comprehensive schools, in well designed buildings in Sawston, Comberton, Cottenham, Bottisham and Linton, among other places.

## ISLEHAM

An uncompromising fen-edge village with the Bedford Level stretching away to the north, there is nothing picturesque about Isleham; its houses and cottages, of whatever period, are practical and workmanlike. It has, however, the remarkable church of St Andrew (see chapter 5) and the priory church of St Margaret of Antioch (chapter 8). Elsewhere in the village are neat little almshouses founded by Lady Peyton, who died in 1518, and to the north there is modern waterside development by Isleham Lock on the river Lark.

## KIMBOLTON

Although in size no more than a large village, Kimbolton has the air of a small and prosperous country town. It was an important centre in medieval times with both a market and a fair. The High Street was the market place until 1890, which explains its generous width. It is lined with handsome seventeenth- and eighteenth-century buildings with no discordant modern intrusions. Kimbolton Castle (chapter 6), at the top of the street, houses the independent Kimbolton School, which also owns several of the larger houses. Parallel to the High Street is East Street, with sixteenth- and seventeenth-century cottages in a sort of irregular harmony, an outstanding example of English domestic building. There are also interesting lanes and alleys. St Andrew's church (chapter 5) stands at the foot of the High Street facing the north pavilion of the castle gatehouse, and a happily positioned cedar tree, at the far end. Later development is tucked away further west so that not even a petrol pump spoils the scene. The sharp bends

59

*The Trinity Guildhall at Linton.*

at either end of the street are the result of re-aligning the highway centuries ago to run through the market place.

## LINTON

The narrow High Street lined with modest cottages leads down to a crossing of the Linton branch of the Cam and then ascends past the beautifully pargeted Chaundlers, the best house in the village. The church is tucked away near the river, a warm and friendly building with much thirteenth- and fourteenth-century work. Close to the church is the early sixteenth-century half-timbered Trinity Guildhall. Linton held a market until the 1860s and still has a Market Lane. A good variety of cottages hides down side streets and there are also a wooden mill, an impressive Congregational church dating from 1818 and some handsome pubs. Linton Zoo (chapter 8) is close by.

## LITTLEPORT

*Early closing Wednesday.*

This small fen town is unexciting architecturally apart from its large fifteenth-century church. There was plenty of excitement, however, in 1816 when the Littleport food riots broke out. Finding their pay inadequate to buy sufficient food to keep their families alive, the men of Littleport armed themselves with guns, punt guns and farm implements and attacked some of the wealthier houses in the town. The vicar fled to Ely

for help; the rioters followed, damaging property but not injuring people. The military were sent for and quelled the riot with great brutality. After a trial five rioters were hanged and five transported, with many more being imprisoned. Local sympathy in general was with the rioters but the Bishop and clergy rejoiced in their defeat. A plaque in St Mary's church, Ely, commemorates the hanged men.

## MADINGLEY

Madingley Hall is a sixteenth-century mansion of quality and importance with many later additions and alterations. Edward VII, then Prince of Wales, stayed here while he was a Cambridge undergraduate and his father, the Prince Consort, became ill when visiting him. Now the hall belongs to Cambridge University. The gateway to the stable court came from the Old Schools in Cambridge, being removed when the library was built in 1754. Madingley has a well known pub, the Three Horseshoes, a mainly fourteenth-century churh, St Mary Magdalene, with a good interior, and a delightful little primary school taken over and successfully run by the parents after the local education authority closed it.

## MARCH

March developed around a crossing of the old river Nene with a market place close by. As the town grew a larger market was established in Broad Street. March became an important railway centre both for passenger interchange and the marshalling of freight; in the early 1930s about two thousand people were employed on the railways here and the Whitemoor yards extended to 68 acres (28 ha). This railway activity has diminished in the 1970s and 1980s and March has also lost its status as county town of the Isle of Ely. It is still a busy fenland business and shopping centre with pleasant walks by the riverside. Note the fanciful George V coronation fountain in Broad Street and the more fanciful town hall of 1900 in the Market Place. There is a local folk museum in the High Street (see chapter 7). The splendid parish church, St Wendreda's, is a mile (1.5 km) south of the town centre (see chapter 5).

## MELBOURN
The village is bisected by the A10 London road. It has a mainly thirteenth-century church, with two top-class restaurants close by, several pleasant cottages and the oldest Baptist chapel in the county, built in about 1716. By contrast a Science Park and other 'high tech' developments have been established on the outskirts. There has been a settlement here since earliest recorded times with prehistoric burial sites to the south and some evidence of Roman occupation.

## MELDRETH
This is a companion village to Melbourn, separated by less than half a mile. The small green at the old village centre has stocks and a whipping post and the base of a medieval cross, all in the shade of a spreading chestnut tree. Holy Trinity church is at the north end; it has a Norman chancel and some good windows. This is a special area for fruit with many orchards around both Melbourn and Meldreth.

## ORWELL
The Royal Commission for Historical Monuments lists 39 buildings in this small village. The High Street and the loop formed by Town Green Road and Back Street provide a fascinating compendium of domestic building from the sixteenth to the nineteenth centuries and more recent additions are generally tactful. St Andrew's church has twelfth-century work although most of the interior is fourteenth-century. The chancel with its wagon roof is especially notable. Clunch, used in the local churches, was once quarried at Orwell. Malton Farm, by the riverside 1¼ miles (2 km) south-east, is originally fifteenth-century and is all that remains of the village of Malton which once included a retreat for the masters and scholars of Christ's College.

## PAPWORTH EVERARD
The early nineteenth-century hall has become famous as a heart transplant hospital. Papworth Village Settlement was founded in 1916 to provide workshops for the employment of disabled people. The church is mostly a Victorian rebuilding.

## PAPWORTH ST AGNES
This is for the most part a nineteenth-century estate village. The old village bakehouse stands on the green. Manor Farm dates from about 1585.

## PARSON DROVE
A few houses scattered along a long straight road is Parson Drove, once a centre of the woad industry. The indigo dye was used in Britain before the Roman invasions but the plant ceased to be cultivated in the late nineteenth century and the last woad mill has long disintegrated. Relics of the industry may be seen in the Wisbech Museum (chapter 7). St John's church is now redundant, but the interior is fine and it is worth a visit. The chancel was destroyed by flooding in 1613.

## PETERBOROUGH
*Early closing Monday and Thursday.*

Both a cathedral city and a designated 'new town', Peterborough has rapidly expanded since the mid 1970s while still preserving much of the best of its past. During the Roman occupation it was an important pottery-making centre and in the Anglo-Saxon period it grew in reputation and wealth following the foundation of a monastery at Medeshamstede on the site where the cathedral, consecrated in 1237, now stands. Peterborough became a diocese in 1541 but the city remained a medium-sized market centre until the coming of the railway age, when it found itself connected to five railway companies including the main Great Northern line. The railways attracted industry as well as setting up their own workshops and housing. A vast brickmaking industry grew up on the outskirts and several heavy engineering undertakings followed. The new town development has replaced these older industries with a wide variety of newer ones, transformed the shopping centre, created larger new residential areas with much improved amenities and leisure facilities, and has imposed a network of fast roads making access to the city centre surprisingly rapid and trouble-free.

Car-parking in Peterborough is comparatively easy and the vast new Queensgate shopping centre is only a few steps from the old city with its market cross or guildhall, fine medieval parish church of St John the Baptist, town hall and, a short distance away, the old custom house by the river Nene. The central area is almost wholly pedestrianised. Across

Cathedral Square from the guildhall is the gateway to the cathedral precincts, framing the splendid west front (see chapter 5).

Close to the centre is the Embankment Arena with indoor and outdoor swimming pools, the Key Theatre, the Wirrina Stadium for sports and concerts, an athletics track and, across the river, the City Station of the Nene Valley Steam Railway (see chapter 8). Within the new town area is the East of England Ice Rink, where international events are held, the 500 acre (200 ha) Ferry Meadows Country Park (see chapter 8), two municipal golf courses and two sports and leisure centres. Peterborough has its own excellent string orchestra and one of the two professional football teams in the county.

## RAMPTON

All Saints' church is one of the few thatched churches in Britain. Much of the building is thirteenth- and fourteenth-century, with some remains of medieval wall painting and a fine Elizabethan pulpit. The village has a green with splendid trees and a small manor house with Dutch gables. East of the church is Giants Hill, the remains of a fort probably dating from the baronial uprisings of the twelfth century.

*The abbey gatehouse at Ramsey.*

## RAMSEY

On this island in the fens an abbey was founded in AD 969. The town developed around the abbey which became of major importance in medieval times. After the Dissolution Ramsey lost much of the reason for its existence and it suffered further from the plague of 1666, which killed over four hundred people, and from major fires in the late seventeenth and eighteenth centuries. Apart from the abbey gatehouse and the mansion on the abbey site almost all the buildings are no older than the nineteenth century. The width of the main street, the Great Whyte, is explained by the fact that a watercourse once ran along the middle of it. Here was a medieval dock serving the abbey and its associated buildings. The Little Whyte had a smaller but similar layout. The watercourse was culverted in the late nineteenth century. The parish church, a harmonious building inside and out, originated as the abbey hospice. It is mostly Norman, although the tower was built in 1672 with stone from the demolished abbey buildings. It contains some Morris glass. Across the green from the church the abbey gatehouse is now owned by the National Trust (admission is free).

**Warboys**, 4 miles (6.5 km) south of Ramsey, was the home of Alice, Agnes and John Samuel, the so-called Witches of Warboys, hanged in 1593 for the murder of Lady Cromwell and the bewitching of the five daughters of Squire Throckmorton. This is an important case in the history of witchcraft in England though there seems little doubt of the Samuels' innocence.

## REACH

This small village, originally an inland port, developed where the Devil's Dyke (chapter 4) meets the old watercourse called Reach Lode, still navigable by shallow craft. Two settlements faced each other across the Dyke but they came together when the earthwork was progressively cut away leaving the present green. The Hythe, a chalk promontory, juts out into the lode and traces of several basins and docks on either side of it may still be discerned. In medieval times Reach exported building materials, mainly clunch, and agricultural produce to Ely, Cambridge and beyond, while a variety of goods for Reach Fair, in existence by 1201 and a major event, were landed here. Trade ceased by 1884. There are the ruins of a chapel and several seventeenth- and eighteenth-century houses. Reach Fair has been revived in a small way and is held every May Day bank holiday.

## ST IVES

Only three chapel bridges survive in England; St Leger's chapel on St Ives bridge was

*The smithy on the green at Thriplow.*

consecrated in 1426. Now that a bypass has removed much of the traffic the bridge is safe to linger on and the chapel key is quickly obtainable — see the notice. St Ives itself grew up on the site of a busy Easter Fair by the village of Slepe (today recalled in the name of the Slepe Hall Hotel), where St Ivo died in the sixth century. The town suffered greatly in the Black Death of 1349 but recovered to become a small market town with, from time to time, a flourishing riverside trade. Oliver Cromwell lived here for several years and is commemorated by a fine statue. The church is mostly fifteenth-century but there are few very old buildings apart from the Manor House in Bridge Street, as much of the town was destroyed by a fire in 1689. The centre is a conservation area and The Lanes, a network of alleyways between Market Hill and the riverside, are well worth exploring. There is a good variety of building styles along the quay, making St Ives one of the most attractive of riverside towns, and a wide selection of small specialist shops with plenty of pubs and restaurants. The Norris Museum (chapter 7) has an excellent local collection. Within easy distance are the pretty riverside villages of Houghton, the Hemingfords and Holywell.

## ST NEOTS

Now that the town is bypassed by both the A1 and the A45 St Neots can be more readily appreciated. It was once the site of an important priory and developed into a major market centre, as can be seen from the extensive market place and the large number of inns, one of which, the Bridge, has a carved stone from the priory set in an outside wall. There has been a river crossing here since 1080 and trade from the Great Ouse contributed to the town's prosperity. Around the market square are several good eighteenth-century buildings. St Mary's church stands on the edge of the town; it has an especially fine tower and much good Perpendicular work, including some excellent screens. A 500 acre (200 ha) riverside park has been developed on the far side of the river and the Ouse provides moorings for a large number of cruisers. The population is now about 22,000, making St Neots the third largest town in the county. The well stocked local museum is housed in the buildings of Longsands School (see chapter 7).

## SAWSTON

This large village 6 miles (9.5 km) south of Cambridge has a long association with the paper-making industry. Two branches of the Cam meet here and their water drove the early paper mills. The church has some good work of the twelfth and thirteenth centuries. Sawston Hall is a distinguished Elizabethan house, a rebuilding of a mansion burnt down in 1553 after Mary Tudor had spent a night there shortly before her accession. Then the hall belonged to the Catholic family of Huddlestone and it contains a well known priest hole. A late eighteenth-century chapel, a long gallery and fine panelling are other features. The hall stands in attractive grounds.

*The Haycock Inn at Wansford.*

## THE SHELFORDS

Great and Little Shelford lie either side of the eastern branch of the Cam. **Great Shelford** is very much a Cambridge suburb but retains some handsome houses and cottages by the river. St Mary's church, apart from the tower, is nearly all early fifteenth-century; special features include a fine angel roof to the nave, good screens and pulpit and a Doom painting over the chancel arch. All Saints' in **Little Shelford** also has fine woodwork and a rare collection of monuments. Next to it is the Priesthouse, a grand example of Victorian Gothic that could have stepped from the pages of Edgar Allan Poe. Little Shelford has suffered less from modern development than its neighbour.

## SHEPRETH

Near the village centre is a handsome mill house. Docwra's Manor (chapter 6) by the crossroads is a fine eighteenth-century house with gardens often open to the public. Manor Farm was originally owned by Chatteris nunnery; some of the buildings date from about 1500. Near the railway station is a fish farm and small wildlife sanctuary. On the road to Barrington is a riverside walk by the Ashwell branch of the Cam.

## SOHAM

This small town, or large village, is rich in history although its present-day attractions are not especially obvious. It grew up beside a lake, Soham Mere, and in the seventh century a cathedral was built here by St Felix across the main street opposite St Andrew's church, which itself stands on the site of an Anglo-Saxon cemetery. For centuries communication was almost entirely by water and even nowadays there is a Ship Inn beside the now insignificant Soham Lode. The causeway to Ely was not made until the twelfth century. The splendid tower of St Andrew's is early fifteenth-century but much of the church is considerably older. It has one of the finest nave roofs in the county. Adjacent to the churchyard is the Fountain Inn with a seventeenth-century steelyard, once used for weighing carts on leaving the market, on the side of the building. Most of the older buildings in Soham are characteristically fenland, making no concessions to such fads as flourish or decoration. Downfield Mill (chapter 4) dates from 1726.

## SUTTON

Sutton-in-the-Isle stands on the southwestern edge of the Isle of Ely with wide views across fenland to the south. From the west end of the village a road runs down to Sutton Gault with a little public house, the Anchor, crouched by the floodbank of the New Bedford River. Here was the experimental hovertrain track, a forward-looking project abandoned for lack of government support. There are some good large houses at the eastern end of Sutton and a very fine church, St Andrew's, built by two Bishops of Ely and virtually complete by 1400. The splendid tower dominates the area; the top two stages derive from the Ely octagon with the design skilfully adapted for this different purpose. In the chancel the Darby memorial window, 1975, is a striking example of modern stained glass.

## SWAFFHAM BULBECK and SWAFFHAM PRIOR

These two fen-edge villages stand a mile (1.6 km) apart some 8 miles (13 km) east of Cambridge. Their names reveal details of their earlier history. 'Swaffham' is the village or estate of the Swabians, early invaders of Britain. 'Bulbeck' refers to Hugh or Hugo of Bolbec, near Harfleur, while 'Prior' was the Prior of Ely. Both Hugh and the Prior were major landowners in these parishes about nine hundred years ago.

Swaffham Bulbeck is a linear village with several fine old houses including Burgh Hall (about 1500), Linton House and Bolebec Cottage, both sixteenth-century and all three timber-framed. St Mary's church is mainly fourteenth-century. Half a mile (800 metres) north is a separate settlement known today as Commercial End but originally called Newnham. This developed as a trading centre near the head of Swaffham Lode. The Merchant's House became the headquarters with its own wharf and counting house, and Thomas Bowyer, who expanded the undertaking in the early nineteenth century, built warehouses and cottages for his workers and agent. There is also an eighteenth-century malting. The single street of Commercial End is a triumph of domestic design and among the most attractive streets in the county. Opposite the northern end is a house called The Abbey, built on the site of a Benedictine priory founded by Isobel de Bolbec. The vaulted undercroft of about 1300 still survives.

Swaffham Prior is notable for its two churches (chapter 5). The older houses stand on the west side of the High Street. Baldwin Manor is one of the finest sixteenth-century houses in the county. Among many charming cottages is one opposite the churchyard that belonged to the poet Edwin Muir. The Cage on Cage Hill is a combined fire-engine house, lock-up and pound, built in 1830. There is a mid-Victorian tower mill above the village.

## THORNEY

In early times this was a major Christian centre with a seventh-century monastery and a collection of its own saints. Thorney is now for the most part a nineteenth-century estate village dominated by a mock-Jacobean water tower. Of the great abbey that succeeded the monastery only a fragment is left (see chapter 5). For over 350 years Thorney was the local seat of the Earls — later Dukes — of Bedford, who lived in the house opposite the abbey. It

was a Duke of Bedford who laid out the estate housing along the main road, a remarkably successful enterprise both in design and for the welfare of his tenants. The water tower, fed by the Thorney River, was a ducal flourish.

*St Mary's church, Whittlesey.*

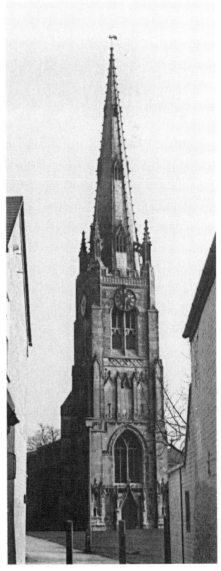

*The guildhall, Whittlesford.*

## THRIPLOW

This is an ancient settlement with iron age barrows (now destroyed) recorded nearby and several more, iron or bronze age, on Thriplow Heath to the south near the Icknield Way. On the heath in 1647 Cromwell's army gathered while its future was discussed. It was eventually decided to continue with the campaign against the King. An old smithy stands on the village green. St George's church was much restored by Sir Gilbert Scott in 1877. A daffodil festival is held here each April and Thriplow Meadows, on the north edge of the village, are open to members of the Cambridge Wildlife Trust and are notable for the summer display of marsh orchids.

## WANSFORD

This riverside village developed where the old Great North Road crosses the river Nene. It has an exceptionally wide main street and a narrow stone bridge. The earliest recorded bridge here was in 1221; the present bridge was built in the 1570s and the navigation arch was added in 1795. As an eighteenth-century river port Wansford imported coal from Newcastle via the Wash and grain, distributed by road to the Midlands, and exported mainly stone from nearby quarries. Today Wansford is notable for the Haycock, a posting house

built in 1632, one of the largest inns of the seventeenth century with stabling for 150 horses, a cockfighting loft and a brewhouse. 'The best of Inns: the bridge, the river, the church beyond, and all about contribute to the right Inn scenery', wrote Viscount Torrington in 1790. Originally called the Swan, the Haycock's name comes from the mythical adventure of drunken Barnaby who fell asleep on a haycock and was carried away by a flood, eventually being cast up at Wansford. This is illustrated on the inn sign and on a much older one preserved above the cooling arch where the post horses once stood to cool down after their journey.

## WHITTLESEY

This small fen town has a spacious and leisurely air about it, except on market day. It has some good seventeenth- and eighteenth-century houses and a fine butter cross in the Market Place close to one of the most handsome Post Office buildings to be found anywhere. The local hero, Sir Harry Smith, one of Wellington's generals, is commemorated by a statue, a chapel in St Mary's church and a public house, the Hero of Aliwal. South of the town is King's Dyke, part of the Middle Level waterway network, where a right-angled bend limits the size of boats navigating between

Nene and Ouse. North is the Roman Fen Causeway. The road to Thorney crosses Morton's Leam, a channel of the Nene cut about 1480, and runs close to the spectacular Dog-in-a-Doublet Sluice on the main river, with a public house at hand. The site of the lake known as Whittlesey Mere is 4 miles (6.5 km) to the south-west. Whittlesey has two churches: the fourteenth-century St Andrew's and St Mary's (chapter 5).

## WHITTLESFORD

This spacious village lies south of Cambridge between the Cam and M11. A carefully restored timbered guildhall stands in the centre. Diagonally opposite is the blue-painted Tickell Arms, a famously idiosyncratic public house. St Andrew's church (see chapter 5) is on the eastern edge of the village with the mill nearby.

## WISBECH

*Early closing Wednesday; market day Thursday and Saturday.*

Once the Well Stream, a channel of the Great Ouse, met the river Nene here and flowed into the sea then only 4 miles (6.5 km) to the north. Churchill Road now marks the line of the old river and of the Wisbech Canal which occupied its bed until the 1940s. Wisbech has always been a port; its prosperity has fluctuated but today it is quite busy though less so than its Norfolk neighbour, King's Lynn. Eighteenth-century prosperity is reflected in the famous Brinks, two rows of handsome mostly Georgian buildings facing each other across the Nene. Outstanding is Peckover House (chapter 6) on North Brink but there are several fine frontages on both sides. Until the floods of 1978 five large warehouses lined the river below the bridge; now only one

The Crescent Wisbech.

67

*The gardens of Peckover House, Wisbech.*

survives. Two other notable areas of the town are the Old Market, west of the river, and the Crescent, part of a scheme by a local builder, Joseph Medworth, in the early years of the nineteenth century. This is a model of town house development and is kept in perfect condition. The Crescent surrounds the site of Wisbech Castle, now represented only by a house of 1816 called Wisbech Castle in Museum Square, used as an educational and administrative centre. The Wisbech Museum (chapter 7) was built in 1846 and across the square is the parish church of St Peter and St Paul.

Other notable features of the town include the memorial to Thomas Clarkson, the leading fighter for the abolition of the slave trade, and the Angles Theatre, dating from 1793 and now restored and reopened. There are Tudor vaults beneath the impressive mainly eight-eenth-century Rose and Crown. Octavia Hill, a founder of the National Trust, was born at 7 South Brink. Had Wisbech been properly by-passed some years ago instead of being made into a traffic junction it would have possessed even more character and interest. Even so it retains in North Brink what Pevsner described as 'one of the most perfect Georgian streets in England' and has a large free central car park so that exploration on foot is both easy and very satisfying.

## WOODHURST

This little village in open country north of St Ives consists of one continuous street oval in shape and lined with cottages. It is of interest as a perfect example of a ring village. It originated in a woodland clearing and the name is first recorded in 1209.

*Leverington: a headstone by the church porch.*

# 12
# Tourist information centres

**Cambridge:** Wheeler Street, Cambridge CB2 3QB. Telephone: 0223 322640.
**Ely:** Public Library, Palace Green, Ely. Telephone: 0353 2062.
**Huntingdon:** The Library, Princes Street, Huntingdon. Telephone: 0480 425831.
**Peterborough:** Town Hall, Bridge Street, Peterborough. Telephone: 0733 63141 or 317336.
**Wisbech:** District Library, Ely Place, Wisbech. Telephone: 0945 583263 or 64009.

# CAMBRIDGESHIRE

* **Nature reserve, etc. (Ch. 2)**
⊓ **Place of archaeological interest (Ch. 4)**
+ **Church or cathedral (Ch. 5)**
▲ **Historic building, garden (Ch. 6)**
M **Museum (Ch. 7)**
O **Other place to visit (Ch. 8)**
W **Windmill or watermill (Ch. 8)**
■ **Town or village (Ch. 11)**

70